Bible 500
Teacher's Guide

CONTENTS

Author: Alpha Omega Staff

Editor: Alan Christopherson, M.S.

Alpha Omega Publications ®

300 North McKemy Avenue, Chandler, Arizona 85226-2618
© MMII by Alpha Omega Publications ® All rights reserved
"LIFEPAC is a registered trademark of Alpha Omega Publications"

OVERVIEW

BIBLE

Curriculum Overview
Grades 1–12

Bible LIFEPAC Overview

	Grade 1	Grade 2	Grade 3
LIFEPAC 1	GOD CREATED ALL THINGS • God created day and night • God created land and sea • God created plants and animals • God created people	WHO AM I? • God made us • God loves me • God helps me • God helped Daniel	WHY AM I HERE? • I love and obey God • I praise God • I worship God • I serve God
LIFEPAC 2	GOD LOVES HIS CHILDREN • God loved Joseph and David • God loved a little slave girl • God, our Father loves us • God's children love Him	THE STORY OF MOSES • Moses in Egypt • Moses in the desert • God talks to Moses • Moses talks to God	THE LIFE OF JESUS • Mary and Joseph • Jesus in the Temple • Jesus teaches and saves • Jesus dies and lives again
LIFEPAC 3	WE CAN PRAY • We can ask and thank God • We can pray God's special prayer • God listens to us • We listen to God	GOD AND YOU • God is great • God keeps his promises • You should obey God • God rewards his people	GOD'S PLAN FOR JOSEPH • The dream of Joseph • Joseph and his brothers • Joseph in Egypt • God watched over Joseph
LIFEPAC 4	GOD WANTS YOU TO BE GOOD • Jesus says love God • God says to love others • You show your love • God says to love yourself	HOW THE BIBLE CAME • Moses and Isaiah • Matthew and Mark • Paul • Bible translators	YOU CAN USE THE BIBLE • The books of the Bible • How to read and study the Bible • How to find verses • How to memorize verses
LIFEPAC 5	OLD TESTAMENT STORIES • Joshua, Daniel, and Jonah • Naomi and Ruth • Abigail and Esther • Isaac, Moses, and David	DAVID'S SLING • David with the sheep • David and the prophet • David and Saul • David and the giant	GOD CARES FOR HIS PEOPLE • God's love for people • God guides people • God protects people • God blesses people
LIFEPAC 6	GOD'S PROMISE • God's Old Testament promises • God's promises kept • The birth of the Promised One • The life of the Promised One	GOD IS EVERYWHERE • Understanding the beginning • Understanding God • The creation • God's will	THE BIBLE, GOD'S WORD • The writers of the Word • The Word is preserved • The Word changes lives • Promises of the Word
LIFEPAC 7	JESUS, OUR SAVIOUR • Jesus taught the people • Jesus healed the people • Jesus saves the people • Jesus will come again	THE STORY OF JOSEPH • Joseph as a boy at home • The worship of Joseph • Joseph in Egypt • Joseph and the famine	ARCHEOLOGY AND THE BIBLE • The search for treasure • Clues from old stories • Explaining the puzzles • Joining the search
LIFEPAC 8	GOD CALLS MISSIONARIES • The woman at the well • Stephen and Paul • Missionaries today • God calls missionaries	GOD AND THE FAMILY • The first family • Abraham's family • Happy families • God's promise to children	THE NEED FOR FRIENDS • We need love • We need friendship • God commands our love • Love for others
LIFEPAC 9	NEW TESTAMENT STORIES • Zacchaeus, Paul, and Peter • Elisabeth and Dorcas • Mary and Martha • Children of the New Testament	GOD MADE THE NATIONS • The people of Babel • God's judgement at Babel • The new nation • Our big world	GOD'S PEOPLE HELP OTHERS • All people are created by God • God loves me • God's love to others • God is my Father
LIFEPAC 10	GOD GAVE YOU MANY GIFTS • God created all things • God loves His children • God gave us His Word • God gave us His Son	GOD, HIS WORD, AND YOU • God as our father • The word of God • Life with God • Belonging to God	GOD'S WORD, JESUS, AND YOU • God speaks to Man • Writers of the Word • Jesus and the Word • God's family

Grade 4	Grade 5	Grade 6	
HOW CAN I LIVE FOR GOD? • Peter found Jesus • Peter Fished for Men • To be born into God's family • To be fruitful through the Spirit	**HOW OTHERS LIVED FOR GOD** • Fellow-laborers with God • Abraham, a man of faith • Servants of God • Co-workers with God	**FROM CREATION TO MOSES** • Creation • The Flood • Abraham and his descendants • Moses and the Law	LIFEPAC 1
GOD'S KNOWLEDGE • Knowledge to create • Learning God's knowledge • The benefits of God's knowledge • Using God's knowledge	**ANGELS** • Characteristics of Angels • Kinds of Angels • The ministry of Angels • Angels in the life of Jesus	**FROM JOSHUA TO SAMUEL** • Conquest and division of the land • The death of Joshua • The Judges of Israel • Ruth, Naomi, and Boaz	LIFEPAC 2
SAUL BEGINS TO LIVE FOR GOD • Saul persecutes the Christians • God changes Saul • Saul preaches about Jesus • Paul belongs to Christ	**THE PRESENCE OF GOD** • Everywhere as God • Everywhere as a person • In the lives of people • In my life	**THE KINGDOM OF ISRAEL** • Samuel and Saul • The reign of David • The reign of Solomon • The books of poetry	LIFEPAC 3
THE BIBLE AND ME • Reading and learning the Bible • Thinking about the Bible • Memorizing the Bible • Living the Bible way	**BIBLE METHODS AND STRUCTURE** • One book with many parts • Books of history • Books of poetry and prophecy • Books of the New Testament	**THE DIVIDED KINGDOM** • From Jeroboam to Captivity • Prophets of Judah and Israel • From Hezekiah to Captivity • Prophets of remaining kingdom	LIFEPAC 4
GOD CARES FOR US • The Twenty-third Psalm • Jesus and the sheep • David as a shepherd • Daniel as a helper	**THE CHRISTIAN IN THE WORLD** • Instruction and correction • Learning correct behavior • Relationships at school • Relationships in the world	**CAPTIVITY AND RESTORATION** • The prophets of the captivity • The returns from exile • The prophets of the Restoration • Creation to Restoration	LIFEPAC 5
HOW CAN I KNOW GOD EXISTS • God's plan for the Jews • A Jewish Saviour • Man searches for God • Man needs God	**PROVING WHAT WE BELIEVE** • The Bible is God's Word • Evidence from the Bible • Evidence from history and science • Knowing that Christ arose	**THE LIFE OF JESUS** • Birth and background • The first years of ministry • The latter years of ministry • The death and Resurrection	LIFEPAC 6
OLD TESTAMENT GEOGRAPHY • Bible Geography • Description of the Land • Abram's Nomadic Life • Abraham's Descendants	**MISSIONARY JOURNEYS OF PAUL** • Paul's background • Paul's missionary journeys • The Jerusalem Council • Paul's last years	**THE FOLLOWERS OF JESUS** • The disciples of Jesus • The friends of Jesus • Miracles of Jesus • The message of Jesus	LIFEPAC 7
GOD–GIVEN WORTH • Who Am I? • God is my Creator • God is my Father • Knowing God's Love	**GOD CREATED MAN FOR ETERNITY** • Preparing for eternity • Christ is our Judge • The judgment of the Christian • The judgment of the unsaved	**THE APOSTLE PAUL** • Paul's background and conversion • Paul's missionary journeys • Paul's letters to churches • Paul's letters to people	LIFEPAC 8
WITNESSING FOR JESUS • Loving God and Others • Following Jesus • Knowing who Jesus is • Following Paul's Example	**AUTHORITY AND LAW** • God is the source of law • The model of law • The authority of the family • Our authority of government	**HEBREWS AND GENERAL EPISTLES** • The book of Hebrews • James and 1st and 2nd Peter • The three Johns • The book of Jude	LIFEPAC 9
GOD'S WAY IS PERFECT • Seeking Knowledge • Science & Geography • Living God's Way • Loving God's Way	**GOD, THE BIBLE, LIVING FOR GOD** • Presence of God and Angels • Understanding the Bible • Areas of service • The order of authority	**REVELATION AND REVIEW** • The Lord Jesus in Revelation • End-time events • Old Testament review • New Testament review	LIFEPAC 10

	Grade 7	Grade 8	Grade 9
LIFEPAC 1	WORSHIP • The nature of worship • Old Testament worship • New Testament worship • True worship	PRAYER • Organization of the Lord's Prayer • Purpose of the Lord's Prayer • History of prayer • Practical use of prayer	THE NEW TESTAMENT • Inter-Testamental period • Pharisees and Sadduces • New Testament themes • New Testament events
LIFEPAC 2	MANKIND • The origin of man • The fall of man • The re-creation of man • The mission of man	SIN AND SALVATION • The nature of sin • The need for salvation • How to receive salvation • The results of salvation	THE GOSPELS • Matthew • Mark • Luke • John
LIFEPAC 3	THE ATTRIBUTES OF GOD • God's nature of love • God's expression of love • The mercy of God • The grace of God	ATTRIBUTES OF GOD • God's justice • God's immutability • God's eternal nature • God's love	THE ACTS OF THE APOSTLES • The writer • The purpose • Pentecost • Missions
LIFEPAC 4	FULFILLED PROPHECIES OF CHRIST • Method of the First Advent • Purpose of the First Advent • The Messiah foretold • Fulfillment of the Messiah	EARLY CHURCH LEADERS • The early church • The church of the Middle Ages • The Renaissance • The Reformation	THE PAULINE EPISTLES • Paul as a person • The early epistles • Prison epistles • The later epistles
LIFEPAC 5	LIVING THE BALANCED LIFE • The Father's gift of life • Man's deception • Fellowship with the Saviour • The life of the Spirit	EARLY CHURCH HISTORY • The Roman Empire • The background of the Jews • The ministry of Jesus • The Jerusalem church	GENERAL EPISTLES • James • First and Second Peter • First, Second, and Third John • Hebrews and Jude
LIFEPAC 6	THE PSALMS • The history of the Psalms • Types of Psalms • Hebrew poetry • Psalm 100	THE EARLY CHURCHES • The church at Antioch • The missionary journeys • The Jerusalem Conference • New Testament churches	THE REVELATION OF JESUS CHRIST • The seven churches • The seven seals and trumpets • The seven signs and plagues • The seven judgments and wonders
LIFEPAC 7	THE LIFE OF CHRIST: PART ONE • Early life of Christ • Christ's ministry begins • The early Judean ministry • The early Galilean ministry	THE BOOK OF PROVERBS • Literary forms and outline • Objectives and purposes • Influence on the New Testament • Key themes	JOB AND SUFFERING • The scenes of Job • Attitudes toward suffering • Christ's suffering on earth • The victory of Christ's suffering
LIFEPAC 8	THE LIFE OF CHRIST: PART TWO • The public ministry in Galilee • The private ministry in Galilee • The Judean ministry • The Perean ministry	TODAY'S PROBLEMS • Guidance for behavior • Characteristics of friendship • Studying effectively • Finding God's will	HOW TO SHARE CHRIST • Personal evangelism • Outreach to others • Personal and family missions • Assisting a missionary
LIFEPAC 9	THE LIFE OF CHRIST: PART THREE • The public Jerusalem ministry • The private Jerusalem ministry • The Crucifixion • The Resurrection	UNDERSTANDING PARENTS • Human parents • Biblical parents • Children's responsibility • Parents and children as a team	GOD'S WILL FOR MY LIFE • The desire of the heart • The Word and work of God • Importance of goals • The use of talents
LIFEPAC 10	IN SUMMARY • The plan of God • Man's history • The Saviour's solution • Worship of Christ	WALKING WITH GOD • Prayer and salvation • The attributes of God • The early church leaders • Christian living	THE WALK WITH CHRIST • Background of the New Testament • The Epistles and Revelation • The importance of suffering • God's will for my life

Grade 10	Grade 11	Grade 12	
CREATION TO ABRAHAM • The six days of creation • The fall of man • Noah and his descendants • Nations of the earth	**THE FAITHFULNESS OF GOD** • Affirmation of God's faithfulness • Nature of God's faithfulness • Manifestations of God's faithfulness • Implications of God's faithfulness	**KNOWING YOURSELF** • Your creation by God • Interacting with others • A child and servant of God • Your personal skills	LIFEPAC 1
ABRAHAM TO MOSES • Abraham's call and promise • The covenant with Isaac • The life of Jacob • Joseph and his family	**ROMANS: PART ONE** • The Roman Empire and Church • The book of Romans • Paul's message to the Romans • Sin and salvation in Romans	**CHRISTIAN MINISTRIES** • Christian ministry defined • Church related ministries • Other ministries • A ministry as a career	LIFEPAC 2
EXODUS AND WANDERINGS • The journey to Sinai • The giving of the Law • Numbering the people • The book of Deuteronomy	**ROMANS: PART TWO** • The chosen of God • Service and submission • From sin to salvation • The victory of salvation	**CHOOSING A CHRISTIAN MINISTRY** • Where to look for a ministry • What to look for in a ministry • How to look for a ministry • Choosing a ministry for a career	LIFEPAC 3
ISRAEL IN CANAAN • Preparing for battle • The fight for the land • Dividing the land • The death of Joshua	**THE DOCTRINE OF JESUS CHRIST** • Identity and incarnation of Christ • The individuality of Christ • Christ's work on the Cross • Christ's work after the Cross	**GODHEAD** • Old Testament view • New Testament view • Historical Perspectives • Faith and man's relationship	LIFEPAC 4
THE JUDGES AND SPIRITUAL DECLINE • Background of Judges • History of the Judges • Examples of spiritual decay • Ruth and redemption	**THE NATION OF ISRAEL** • The covenant with Abraham • Israel as a nation • Old Testament archaeology • New Testament archaeology	**ATTRIBUTES OF GOD** • The Holiness of God • The Goodness of God • Holiness and the believer • Goodness and the Creation	LIFEPAC 5
THE KINGDOM • Samuel and Saul • David • Solomon • Hebrew poetry	**HISTORY OF THE CANON** • Revelation and inspiration • Illumination and interpretation • Authority of the Bible • Formation of the Bible	**THE EPISTLES OF JAMES** • James the man • The message of James • John the man • The message of John's epistles	LIFEPAC 6
THE DIVIDED KINGDOM • Jeroboam to Ahab • Ahab to Jehu • Jehu to Assyrian captivity • Prophets of the period	**FRIENDSHIP, DATING, AND MARRIAGE** • Meaning and role of friendship • Perspectives of dating • Principles of relationships • The structure of marriage	**DANIEL** • A man of conviction • An interpreter of dreams • A watchman in prayer • A man of visions	LIFEPAC 7
THE REMAINING KINGDOM • The time of Hezekiah • Manasseh to Josiah • Jehoahaz to the exile • Prophets of the period	**THE PURSUIT OF HAPPINESS** • Solomon's splendor and sin • Solomon's search • God's solution and action • Solomon's response	**COMPARATIVE RELIGIONS** • Elements of Christianity • The validity of Christian faith • World religions • The occult	LIFEPAC 8
THE CAPTIVITY • Prophets of the period • Jeremiah • Ezekiel • Daniel	**ANSWERS FOR AGNOSTICS** • Integrity of the Bible • Doctrines of the Bible • Interpretation of the Bible • Application of the Bible	**WISDOM FOR TODAY'S YOUTH** • Life and character of David • Life and riches of Solomon • Psalms and Proverbs • The Bible and literature	LIFEPAC 9
THE RESTORATION • First return from exile • The Jews preserved • Second return from exile • Haggai, Zechariah, and Malachi	**GOD, HIS WORD, AND THE CHRISTIAN** • The uniqueness of the Bible • History of Israel • God revealed in the Bible • Principles for living	**PRACTICAL CHRISTIAN LIVING** • Christian fundamentals • Growing in Christian maturity • A ministry for Christ • A testimony for Christ	LIFEPAC 10

MANAGEMENT

STRUCTURE OF THE LIFEPAC CURRICULUM

The LIFEPAC curriculum is conveniently structured to provide one teacher handbook containing teacher support material with answer keys and ten student worktexts for each subject at grade levels two through twelve. The worktext format of the LIFEPACs allows the student to read the textual information and complete workbook activities all in the same booklet. The easy to follow LIFEPAC numbering system lists the grade as the first number(s) and the last two digits as the number of the series. For example, the Language Arts LIFEPAC at the 6th grade level, 5th book in the series would be LA 605.

Each LIFEPAC is divided into 3 to 5 sections and begins with an introduction or overview of the booklet as well as a series of specific learning objectives to give a purpose to the study of the LIFEPAC. The introduction and objectives are followed by a vocabulary section which may be found at the beginning of each section at the lower levels, at the beginning of the LIFEPAC in the middle grades, or in the glossary at the high school level. Vocabulary words are used to develop word recognition and should not be confused with the spelling words introduced later in the LIFEPAC. The student should learn all vocabulary words before working the LIFEPAC sections to improve comprehension, retention, and reading skills.

Each activity or written assignment has a number for easy identification, such as 1.1. The first number corresponds to the LIFEPAC section and the number to the right of the decimal is the number of the activity.

Teacher checkpoints, which are essential to maintain quality learning, are found at various locations throughout the LIFEPAC. The teacher should check 1) neatness of work and penmanship, 2) quality of understanding (tested with a short oral quiz), 3) thoroughness of answers (complete sentences and paragraphs, correct spelling, etc.), 4) completion of activities (no blank spaces), and 5) accuracy of answers as compared to the answer key (all answers correct).

The self test questions are also number coded for easy reference. For example, 2.015 means that this is the 15th question in the self test of Section II. The first number corresponds to the LIFEPAC section, the zero indicates that it is a self test question, and the number to the right of the zero the question number.

The LIFEPAC test is packaged at the centerfold of each LIFEPAC. It should be removed and put aside before giving the booklet to the student for study.

Answer and test keys have the same numbering system as the LIFEPACs and appear at the back of this handbook. The student may be given access to the answer keys (not the test keys) under teacher supervision so that he can score his own work.

A thorough study of the Curriculum Overview by the teacher before instruction begins is essential to the success of the student. The teacher should become familiar with expected skill mastery and understand how these grade level skills fit into the overall skill development of the curriculum. The teacher should also preview the objectives that appear at the beginning of each LIFEPAC for additional preparation and planning.

TEST SCORING and GRADING

Answer keys and test keys give examples of correct answers. They convey the idea, but the student may use many ways to express a correct answer. The teacher should check for the essence of the answer, not for the exact wording. Many questions are high level and require thinking and creativity on the part of the student. Each answer should be scored based on whether or not the main idea written by the student matches the model example. "Any Order" or "Either Order" in a key indicates that no particular order is necessary to be correct.

Most self tests and LIFEPAC tests at the lower elementary levels are scored at 1 point per answer; however, the upper levels may have a point system awarding 2 to 5 points for various answers or questions. Further, the total test points will vary; they may not always equal 100 points. They may be 78, 85, 100, 105, etc.

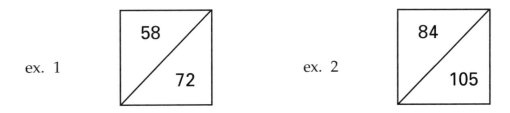

A score box similar to ex.1 above is located at the end of each self test and on the front of the LIFEPAC test. The bottom score, 72, represents the total number of points possible on the test. The upper score, 58, represents the number of points your student will need to receive an 80% or passing grade. If you wish to establish the exact percentage that your student has achieved, find the total points of his correct answers and divide it by the bottom number (in this case 72.) For example, if your student has a point total of 65, divide 65 by 72 for a grade of 90%. Referring to ex. 2, on a test with a total of 105 possible points, the student would have to receive a minimum of 84 correct points for an 80% or passing grade. If your student has received 93 points, simply divide the 93 by 105 for a percentage grade of 86%. Students who receive a score below 80% should review the LIFEPAC and retest using the appropriate Alternate Test found in the Teacher's Guide.

The following is a guideline to assign letter grades for completed LIFEPACs based on a maximum total score of 100 points.

LIFEPAC Test = 60% of the Total Score (or percent grade)
Self Test   = 25% of the Total Score (average percent of self tests)
Reports   = 10% or 10* points per LIFEPAC
Oral Work   = 5% or 5* points per LIFEPAC
*Determined by the teacher's subjective evaluation of the student's daily work.

Example:

LIFEPAC Test Score	=	92%	92 x .60	=	55 points
Self Test Average	=	90%	90 x .25	=	23 points
Reports				=	8 points
Oral Work				=	4 points

TOTAL POINTS = 90 points

Grade Scale based on point system:

100	–	94	=	A
93	–	86	=	B
85	–	77	=	C
76	–	70	=	D
Below		70	=	F

TEACHER HINTS and STUDYING TECHNIQUES

LIFEPAC Activities are written to check the level of understanding of the preceding text. The student may look back to the text as necessary to complete these activities; however, a student should never attempt to do the activities without reading (studying) the text first. Self tests and LIFEPAC tests are never open book tests.

Language arts activities (skill integration) often appear within other subject curriculum. The purpose is to give the student an opportunity to test his skill mastery outside of the context in which it was presented.

Writing complete answers (paragraphs) to some questions is an integral part of the LIFEPAC Curriculum in all subjects. This builds communication and organization skills, increases understanding and retention of ideas, and helps enforce good penmanship. Complete sentences should be encouraged for this type of activity. Obviously, single words or phrases do not meet the intent of the activity, since multiple lines are given for the response.

Review is essential to student success. Time invested in review where review is suggested will be time saved in correcting errors later. Self tests, unlike the section activities, are closed book. This procedure helps to identify weaknesses before they become too great to overcome. Certain objectives from self tests are cumulative and test previous sections; therefore, good preparation for a self test must include all material studied up to that testing point.

The following procedure checklist has been found to be successful in developing good study habits in the LIFEPAC curriculum.

1. Read the introduction and Table of Contents.
2. Read the objectives.
3. Recite and study the entire vocabulary (glossary) list.
4. Study each section as follows:
    a. Read the introduction and study the section objectives.
    b. Read all the text for the entire section, but answer none of the activities.
    c. Return to the beginning of the section and memorize each vocabulary word and definition.
    d. Reread the section, complete the activities, check the answers with the answer key, correct all errors, and have the teacher check.
    e. Read the self test but do not answer the questions.
    f. Go to the beginning of the first section and reread the text and answers to the activities up to the self test you have not yet done.
    g. Answer the questions to the self test without looking back.
    h. Have the self test checked by the teacher.
    i. Correct the self test and have the teacher check the corrections.
    j. Repeat steps a–i for each section.

5. Use the SQ3R* method to prepare for the LIFEPAC test.
6. Take the LIFEPAC test as a closed book test.
7. LIFEPAC tests are administered and scored under direct teacher supervision. Students who receive scores below 80% should review the LIFEPAC using the SQ3R* study method and take the Alternate Test located in the Teacher Handbook. The final test grade may be the grade on the Alternate Test or an average of the grades from the original LIFEPAC test and the Alternate Test.

    *SQ3R: Scan the whole LIFEPAC,
        Question yourself on the objectives,
        Read the whole LIFEPAC again,
        Recite through an oral examination, and
        Review weak areas.

GOAL SETTING and SCHEDULES

Each school must develop its own schedule, because no single set of procedures will fit every situation. The following is an example of a daily schedule that includes the five LIFEPAC subjects as well as time slotted for special activities.

Possible Daily Schedule

8:15	–	8:25	Pledges, prayer, songs, devotions, etc.
8:25	–	9:10	Bible
9:10	–	9:55	Language Arts
9:55	–	10:15	Recess (juice break)
10:15	–	11:00	Mathematics
11:00	–	11:45	Social Studies
11:45	–	12:30	Lunch, recess, quiet time
12:30	–	1:15	Science
1:15	–		Drill, remedial work, enrichment*

*Enrichment: Computer time, physical education, field trips, fun reading, games and puzzles, family business, hobbies, resource persons, guests, crafts, creative work, electives, music appreciation, projects.

Basically, two factors need to be considered when assigning work to a student in the LIFEPAC curriculum.

The first is time. An average of 45 minutes should be devoted to each subject, each day. Remember, this is only an average. Because of extenuating circumstances a student may spend only 15 minutes on a subject one day and the next day spend 90 minutes on the same subject.

The second factor is the number of pages to be worked in each subject. A single LIFEPAC is designed to take 3 to 4 weeks to complete. Allowing about 3-4 days for LIFEPAC introduction, review, and tests, the student has approximately 15 days to complete the LIFEPAC pages. Simply take the number of pages in the LIFEPAC, divide it by 15 and you will have the number of pages that must be completed on a daily basis to keep the student on schedule. For example, a LIFEPAC containing 45 pages will require 3 completed pages per day. Again, this is only an average. While working a 45 page LIFEPAC, the student may complete only 1 page the first day if the text has a lot of activities or reports, but go on to complete 5 pages the next day.

Long range planning requires some organization. Because the traditional school year originates in the early fall of one year and continues to late spring of the following year, a calendar should be devised that covers this period of time. Approximate beginning and completion dates can be noted on the calendar as well as special occasions such as holidays, vacations and birthdays. Since each LIFEPAC takes 3-4 weeks or eighteen days to complete, it should take about 180 school days to finish a set of ten LIFEPACs. Starting at the beginning school date, mark off eighteen school days on the calendar and that will become the targeted completion date for the first LIFEPAC. Continue marking the calendar until you have established dates for the remaining nine LIFEPACs making adjustments for previously noted holidays and vacations. If all five subjects are being used, the ten established target dates should be the same for the LIFEPACs in each subject.

FORMS

The sample weekly lesson plan and student grading sheet forms are included in this section as teacher support materials and may be duplicated at the convenience of the teacher.

The student grading sheet is provided for those who desire to follow the suggested guidelines for assignment of letter grades found on page 3 of this section. The student's self test scores should be posted as percentage grades. When the LIFEPAC is completed the teacher should average the self test grades, multiply the average by .25 and post the points in the box marked self test points. The LIFEPAC percentage grade should be multiplied by .60 and posted. Next, the teacher should award and post points for written reports and oral work. A report may be any type of written work assigned to the student whether it is a LIFEPAC or additional learning activity. Oral work includes the student's ability to respond orally to questions which may or may not be related to LIFEPAC activities or any type of oral report assigned by the teacher. The points may then be totaled and a final grade entered along with the date that the LIFEPAC was completed.

The Student Record Book which was specifically designed for use with the Alpha Omega curriculum provides space to record weekly progress for one student over a nine week period as well as a place to post self test and LIFEPAC scores. The Student Record Books are available through the current Alpha Omega catalog; however, unlike the enclosed forms these books are not for duplication and should be purchased in sets of four to cover a full academic year.

WEEKLY LESSON PLANNER

Week of:

Subject	Subject	Subject	Subject
Monday			
Subject	Subject	Subject	Subject
Tuesday			
Subject	Subject	Subject	Subject
Wednesday			
Subject	Subject	Subject	Subject
Thursday			
Subject	Subject	Subject	Subject
Friday			

WEEKLY LESSON PLANNER

Week of:

	Subject	Subject	Subject	Subject
Monday				
	Subject	Subject	Subject	Subject
Tuesday				
	Subject	Subject	Subject	Subject
Wednesday				
	Subject	Subject	Subject	Subject
Thursday				
	Subject	Subject	Subject	Subject
Friday				

Student Name _____   Year _____

Bible

LP #	Self Test Scores by Sections					Self Test Points	LIFEPAC Test	Oral Points	Report Points	Final Grade	Date
	1	2	3	4	5						
01											
02											
03											
04											
05											
06											
07											
08											
09											
10											

History & Geography

LP #	Self Test Scores by Sections					Self Test Points	LIFEPAC Test	Oral Points	Report Points	Final Grade	Date
	1	2	3	4	5						
01											
02											
03											
04											
05											
06											
07											
08											
09											
10											

Language Arts

LP #	Self Test Scores by Sections					Self Test Points	LIFEPAC Test	Oral Points	Report Points	Final Grade	Date
	1	2	3	4	5						
01											
02											
03											
04											
05											
06											
07											
08											
09											
10											

Student Name _____   Year _____

Mathematics

LP #	Self Test Scores by Sections 1	2	3	4	5	Self Test Points	LIFEPAC Test	Oral Points	Report Points	Final Grade	Date
01											
02											
03											
04											
05											
06											
07											
08											
09											
10											

Science

LP #	Self Test Scores by Sections 1	2	3	4	5	Self Test Points	LIFEPAC Test	Oral Points	Report Points	Final Grade	Date
01											
02											
03											
04											
05											
06											
07											
08											
09											
10											

Spelling/Electives

LP #	Self Test Scores by Sections 1	2	3	4	5	Self Test Points	LIFEPAC Test	Oral Points	Report Points	Final Grade	Date
01											
02											
03											
04											
05											
06											
07											
08											
09											
10											

TEACHER

NOTES

INSTRUCTIONS FOR BIBLE

The LIFEPAC curriculum from grades two through twelve is structured so that the daily instructional material is written directly into the LIFEPACs. The student is encouraged to read and follow this instructional material in order to develop independent study habits. The teacher should introduce the LIFEPAC to the student, set a required completion schedule, complete teacher checks, be available for questions regarding both content and procedures, administer and grade tests, and develop additional learning activities as desired. Teachers working with several students may schedule their time so that students are assigned to a quiet work activity when it is necessary to spend instructional time with one particular student.

The Teacher Notes section of the handbook lists the required or suggested materials for the LIFEPACs and provides additional learning activities for the students. The materials section refers only to LIFEPAC materials and does not include materials which may be needed for the additional activities. Additional learning activities provide a change from the daily school routine, encourage the student's interest in learning and may be used as a reward for good study habits.

Materials Needed for LIFEPAC

Required: Suggested:
Bible   Bible atlas
                                             large map showing Paul's missionary journeys

Additional Learning Activities

Section I – Believers in God

1. Help students understand that:
   a. God wants us to become His co-workers after we know Him as our Savior.
   b. Each person has a special task which God wants that person to perform.
   c. We can possess the same character traits that made these Bible characters successful in living for God.
   d. We should recognize these traits and work to develop them in our own lives.
2. Discuss these questions with your student(s).
   a. How has God planned to have His work accomplished?
   b. Who does God want to be His "co-worker"?
   c. How was living for God different for those living in Old Testament times?
   d. Why do people serve God?
   e. How is living for God today the same as it was for those in the Old Testament times?
   f. How and by whom is Abraham honored?
   g. Abraham obeyed God and went to Canaan. What do you think Abraham might have done when he found the war-like nations?
   h. What did Abraham do that did not please God?
   i. How was Abraham pleasing to God?
   j. How do you think Abraham's attitude helped him through all his tests?
   k. What does it mean to be a man (or woman) after God's own heart? How can I be that kind of person?
3. Present the option of a few students performing a puppet show or skit about Abraham's calling by God.
4. Present the option of using construction paper to make individual mottoes about living for God.
5. Using a large map, have the student(s) trace Abraham's journey throughout his life. Identify sites of major happenings in his life.
6. Have a discussion about faith and the role of patience when waiting for God's promises to be fulfilled.

Section II – Servants of God

1. Discuss these questions with your student(s).
   a. How does God use different kinds of people?
   b. Why was Paul able to have such a strong influence on the world?
   c. How did Paul's early life influence his adult life (his trade and witness)?
   d. What is one of the best things you can do to prepare yourself to be a co-worker with God?
   e. Why did Paul persecute the Christians?
   f. What was Paul's first question after his conversion?

    g. What was the main method by which Paul's witness to the Gentile nations was accomplished?

    h. Why did God and the people love David?

    i. Why do you think David refused to wear a helmet and armor when he fought Goliath?

    j. Why do you think David did not kill Saul when he had the opportunity?

    k. Why was the apostle John so close to Jesus?

    l. Why did Jesus call James and John "Sons of Thunder"?

    m. How did John's character change over the years?

2. **Option:** Have the students write and present a short drama about Paul's conversion.

3. **Option:** The students may design personal posters with character traits depicted or illustrated on them.

4. A student may write a report on a Biblical character who lived for God.

Section III – Followers of Jesus

1. Discuss these questions with your student(s).

    a. Why did Noah find grace in the eyes of the Lord?

    b. What was the first thing Noah did when he left the ark?

    c. What was God's promise to Noah?

    d. Why did Elimelech and Naomi leave Judah?

    e. How did Ruth show her love to Naomi?

    f. How did God bless Ruth?

    g. Why did the Lord bless Hannah?

    h. Why did Jonah run from the Lord?

    i. What object lesson did God use to show Jonah that he was wrong?

    j. Why did Jesus have to correct Peter?

    k. Why do you think Peter became a leader in the church?

    l. How did Peter's character change over the years?

    m. Who is your favorite Bible "co-worker" with God? Why?

2. Make a classroom banner using butcher paper or fabric. This activity may be done with several students or as a family. Choose a motto from this LIFEPAC. Some suggestions might be: "Trust and Obey," "For to me to live is Christ," or "Behold the Lamb of God." You may want to pray about it and decide on one of your own. Have one person do the lettering, another the art work, and let all help in gluing letters and pictures on the banner.

3. Make a mural or bulletin board entitled, "A Cloud of Witnesses." Include names of people, places, and Scripture quotations.

4. A student may list some Bible characters who possessed the character traits listed in Section III of the LIFEPAC.

5. A student may interview someone he knows who lives for God and present an oral or written report on the interview.

6. To help students learn about the different Bible co-workers, make a "matching game." To do this, write the Bible co-worker's name on one card. On another card, write one or several outstanding things associated with that person. Have the students try to correctly match all the cards. The cards may be decorated and covered with clear contact paper for lasting use.

Materials Needed for LIFEPAC

Required: Suggested:
Bible   Bible concordance

Additional Learning Activities

Section I – Angels Are Real

1. Discuss these questions with your student(s).
   a. Are angels real?
   b. Has anyone ever seen an angel?
   c. Do angels help us today?
   d. Do people ever become angels?
   e. What do angels do?
   f. What is one of the ministries of angels?
   g. What are some of the things angels can do that people cannot do?
   h. Can you see angels?
   i. Are angels happy?
   j. Are angels wise?
   k. Are all angels alike?
   l. Do very many angels exist?
   m. Are all angels good angels?
2. List all the characteristics and qualities angels have.
3. Draw pictures of how you believe angels look.
4. Some students may re-enact the scene between Gabriel and Mary where Gabriel announces that Mary will have a son, the Son of God, Jesus.

Section II – Angels in the Lives of People

1. Discuss these questions with your student(s).
   a. How does God use angels for messengers?
   b. Who protects Jesus Christ?
   c. What did the angel tell Abraham?
   d. Could angels have delivered Jesus from the Cross?
   e. How did an angel speak to Moses?
   f. How does God use angels to protect men?
   g. How did God use angels to protect Elisha?
   h. How did God use an angel to protect Hezekiah?
   i. How did an angel help Daniel?
   j. How did an angel help Peter and his crew?
   k. How did angels help the children of Israel?
   l. How did the angel direct Philip?
   m. How did God use an angel to supply Elijah's needs?
2. Make a list of all the ways angels help men or serve God as recorded in the Bible.
3. Students may write short stories on how it might have felt to wrestle with the Lord, as did Jacob (Genesis 32:24).
4. Have each student choose a Bible account of when an angel intervened in the life of someone (Moses, Daniel, Philip, Jesus, etc...) and write a "newspaper article" about

how he/she thinks the event may have taken place. Compile all the finished articles into one main "special edition newspaper" about angels in the lives of God's people. You may make enough copies for each student to have his own "newspaper," or just have one class copy.

Section III – Angels in the Life of Jesus

1. Discuss these questions with your student(s).
   a. How did angels minister in Jesus' life?
   b. When did angels begin to work in Jesus' life?
   c. What message did Gabriel have for Zacharias?
   d. What message did Gabriel have for Mary?
   e. What is the difference between how Zacharias reacted to Gabriel's message versus how Mary reacted to her message?
   f. How did an angel appear to Joseph?
   g. How did an angel appear to shepherds in the field?
   h. What message did an angel bring Joseph and Mary?
   i. How did an angel strengthen Jesus in the garden of Gethsemane?
   j. Why did Jesus not call legions of angels to rescue Him from the Cross?
   k. Who rolled the stone away from Jesus' tomb and frightened the guards?
   l. What did Mary Magdalene see when she returned to the tomb?

2. Students may bring in pictures that show angels. Discuss what the angels are doing.

3. Share a missionary story or other stories which tell about how angels have helped God's people.

4. Think of and discuss with the student(s) how people generally view angels and/or how angels are portrayed in stories and on television. Based on what we know about angels from God's word, is this a true perception? Why or why not?

5. Allow each student to read a book about angels which has been approved by the teacher and do a written or oral report. Have students include in their reports why they chose the book they did.

6. Discuss songs which have been written about angels. List them briefly and tell what you think they mean.

7. Have students write a story about an encounter with an angel. They may make up their own account or may pretend that they are a Bible character to whom an angel appeared. Stories may be shared and discussed.

Materials Needed for LIFEPAC

Required:
Bible

Suggested:
world map
globe
maps of Eastern U.S., Africa & China
map of Bible lands in Biblical times
picture or model of the Tabernacle
pictures of Daniel's fiery furnace & Jesus walking on water
pictures illustrating Psalm 23

Additional Learning Activities

Section I – God's Presence

1. Discuss these questions with your student(s).
   a. How would you feel if you knew God was not omnipresent?
   b. What are some things that you would do differently if you always were aware that God was present?
   c. Explain to the students that anything which we place before God in our lives is considered to be an idol. What kinds of "idols" do people worship today? How are these idols the same or different from the idols of wood or stone mentioned in the Bible?
   d. Teach your students to recite the "Shema" in Hebrew. The "Shema" (Hebrew for "Hear") is the Jewish confession of faith. It is found in Deuteronomy 6:4-9.

   Sh'ma Yisrael,
   Adonai, Eloheinu,
   Adonai echad.

   Hear, O Israel,
   the Lord our God,
   The Lord is One.

   e. Why was it necessary for Moses to teach the Israelites the Shema? (The Shema was given to guard against the false idol worship of multiple gods which was widely believed among the surrounding nations.)
   f. How would you try to prove to someone else that God is always present?
2. Dramatize the story of Nancy and Cindy (taken from question 1.8 of text).
3. Conduct a panel discussion on the topic, "The Omnipresence of God."
4. Write a short story to show that God is present.
5. List ten different kinds of needs and problems which God could be asked to respond to at the same time around the world.
6. Make a list of what would happen if God was not omnipresent.
7. Keep a diary for one week, recording events that proved God's presence with you.
8. Find other Bible people who proved the presence of God in their lives.
9. Write a poem (or song) about God's presence.

10. Interview various people concerning their experiences of God's presence in their lives.
11. Make a list of activities, sports, or jobs in which it helps the participants to know that God is present.

Section II – God's Presence in the Lives of People

1. Discuss these questions with your student(s).
   a. Why does God show His presence in different ways to different people?
   b. How has God shown His presence in different ways at different times in history?
   c. Why do some people live as if God were not present?
   d. Why do you think missionaries often experience the presence of God more personally than other people?
   e. Why do you think God allows some of His servants to suffer if He is always present with them?
   f. What are some ways God shows His presence in nature and the social world around us?
2. Dramatize events in the lives of Bible or post-Bible people depicting the presence of God in their lives.
3. Dramatize an interview with "Bible characters" or "post-Bible characters" about the presence of God.
4. Read and report on other people who proved the presence of God.
5. Trace the activities of Livingstone, Brainerd, and Gladys Aylward on a map of the world.
6. Draw a map of the travels of these people.
7. Make a diorama of an event in the life of a Bible or a post-Bible person.

Section III – God's Presence in My Life

1. Discuss these questions with your student(s).
   a. Why is God described as having eyes and ears if He is a Spirit and is present everywhere?
   b. How do you think your conscience is a proof that God is present everywhere?
   c. When Jesus was living on the earth, was He omnipresent like God the Father?
   d. What do you think is the most important thing God can do for you because He is always present with you?
   e. How does an omnipresent God help you more than your friends or even your family?
   f. Do you think young people are more or less aware of the presence of God than older people? Why or why not?
   g. What are some things you can do or practice that will make you more aware that God is always present with you?
2. Draw group pictures or murals showing how God was present with people, using, for example, Psalm 23 or the disciples on the Sea of Galilee.
3. Practice a hymn or chorus about the presence of God and sing it individually or together as a class.
4. Make a chart depicting the different ways God has shown His presence to you. For example: hearing, seeing, speaking, forgiving, providing, keeping, or protecting
5. Find and write ten Bible verses that give God's promise of His presence.

6. Study today's newspaper. Find some events that might have been different if the people involved had realized that God was present.
7. Make a collection of sayings, hymns, and poems that expresses something about the presence of God. Make a decorative cover for your booklet. (This can be done individually, or together as one large "scrapbook.")

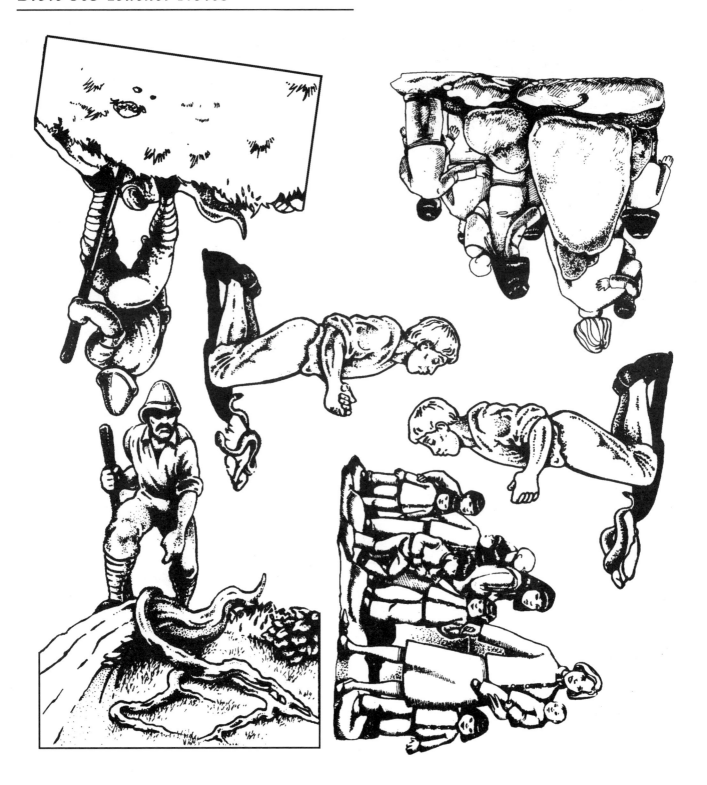

Directions: Paste the whole sheet on heavy white construction paper, lightweight cardboard, or tagboard. Cut the figures apart; then cut carefully and accurately around each figure or group of figures. Paste the front view to the back view, matching the figures accurately, with two T-pins or needles in between. Make the pointed ends of the pins or needles extend below the figure one-quarter inch. Make a papier-mâché mountain or woods scene in which to stand the figures.

Materials Needed for LIFEPAC

Required:

Suggested:
map of the world
globe
map of the Middle East
map of Bible lands
pictures of a house, tree, automobile, school
tag board to construct charts
illustrations of ancient writing
charts of Bible books
time line of Bible chronology

Additional Learning Activities

Section I – The Bible

1. Discuss these questions.
   a. What do you think would happen if forty authors tried to write the same book?
   b. How does the Old Testament tell about Christ before He was born?
2. Participate in a sword drill finding verses of the Old and New Testament.
3. Participate in a debate or panel discussion proving the Bible is one book with related parts.
4. Make memorization cards for Bible verses.

Section II – The Old Testament

1. Discuss these questions.
   a. Can you tell from the name of any of the Old Testament books what the topic of the book might be?
   b. Why do you think it is important to memorize the books of the Bible and verses from the Bible?
2. Make a Bible game. Design cards of Bible books with clues on one side and the name of the book on the other side. Write rules for playing the game.
3. Write a poem or a song using the books of the Old Testament.

Section III – The New Testament

1. Discuss these questions.
   a. How can John 3:16 be called the key to the New Testament and to the whole Bible?
   b. Why do you think the four Gospels were placed first in the New Testament?
2. Design cards of the New Testament books with clues on one side and the name of the books on the other.
3. Write a letter to a friend explaining the purpose of the New Testament.

Materials Needed for LIFEPAC

Required: Suggested:
Bible   None

Additional Learning Activities

Section I – Relationships in the Home

1. Read a story involving a home situation, preferably with a "problem." Discuss the solution or decisions necessary by different family members.
2. Show a video, film, or teaching picture of family life. Ask the children to write as many questions as they can about the showing and family situations. Questions should involve causes or consequences of the family actions or concepts in the picture.
3. Invite a Christian couple to discuss their roles as parents and the interactions and activities they have with their children.
4. Role play situations in the home such as mealtime family discussions, decision-making about family situations, or taking responsibility.
5. Keep a diary for two weeks. Detail in this diary special things that were noteworthy that happened around your home. You might include problem-solving, heart-to-heart talks with Mom or Dad, and exciting experiences.

Section II – Relationships in the Church

1. Have a discussion on how the church is like a family. Also discuss how the church is different from a family.
2. Invite a pastor of a church to talk about relationships in the church.
3. Role play interactions among church members showing each of the characteristics describing love in 1 Corinthians 13:4-7.
4. Discuss with your parents the ways your family might give more support — spiritual and material — to those in need at your church. Share these ideas with other students as a class discussion.

Section III – Relationships in the School

1. Conduct a brainstorming session entitled, "Ways to make our room or school a more Christian place." This may be done by the class as a whole or in small groups, with the results of small group discussion shared later with the whole class.
2. Appoint "detectives" each week to record instances of good behavior, attitudes, and conversation. Share findings once a week, with no names being used (unless the teacher believes that it would be good to also share the names with the positive actions).
3. Divide the class into groups of five or six. Decide on a character trait or habit to portray. Pantomime this trait or habit and let the class guess what the trait is.
4. Have the students give speeches as to what they believe a Christian student's conduct should be at certain times under a given set of circumstances.

Section IV – Relationships in the World of Work

1. Invite someone from the community to share how Christian habits and traits have been applied in daily work situations.

2. Invite a Christian business owner to share about important Christian business principles.

3. Lead a discussion on the relative importance of Christian traits in the world of work. List the choices on the board. Vote to determine the order of their importance.

4. Divide the class into groups. Let each group choose a particular occupation or profession. Each group will list the traits that might be the most important and appropriate in that work or profession. Discuss the reasons for the choices and present the results to the class.

5. Develop a bulletin board showing a Bible verse relating Christian traits in the world of work.

Bible 506 Teacher Notes
_____

Materials Needed for LIFEPAC

Required: Suggested:
Bible   None

Additional learning Activities

Section I – The Bible Is God's Word
1. Conduct a debate, pro and con, on: Is the Bible the Word of God?" Choose carefully those who will take the negative side and explain their position to the class.
2. Invite a Christian archaeologist, historian, or scientist to class to discuss why they believe the Bible to be the Word of God. Alternatively, especially for home-schoolers, take a field trip to attend a lecture or public/private meeting with one of these people.
3. Divide the class into groups. Conduct a "sword drill" from the Bible with groups competing, using verses related to God speaking, prophecy and its fulfillment, or Jesus' quotations from the Old Testament as references.
4. Write a one-page report on reasons why you believe the Bible to be the Word of God.
5. Choose one Old Testament book or one of the four Gospels and list as many times as you can find that God spoke or that Jesus claimed God spoke.

Section II – God Created the World
1. Invite a Christian astronomer or other scientists to present a Biblical view of Creation. Alternatively, especially for home-schoolers, take a field trip to attend a lecture or public/private meeting with one of these people.
2. Show a video or film showing a Creationist view of Creation.
3. Divide the class into three groups. Assign one to research the subject of geology in relation to Creation, another astronomy, another biology. Ask them to report their findings to the class. NOTE: Much material is available on the Internet to help with this research.
4. Write a one-page report on why you could not accept the theory of evolution.
5. List as many questions as you can that would be impossible to answer apart from belief in God's Creation of the Universe.

Section III – Christ Arose from the Dead
1. Lead a discussion comparing the Resurrection and post-Resurrection appearances with other historical events to show that the Resurrection was a historical event.
2. Present a flannelgraph lesson of Paul meeting the risen Christ on the road to Damascus. Show how such a personal experience was necessary to become an apostle.
3. Divide the class into groups. Let each student select an episode connected with the Resurrection or post-Resurrection events. Organize, practice, and present a dramatization of that event.
4. Write a one-page report of what would happen if Jesus had not risen.
5. List all the verses in the book of Acts that refer to the Resurrection.

Materials Needed for LIFEPAC

Required: Suggested:
Bible
concordance
world almanac

Additional Learning Activities

Section I – Paul's Preparation

1. Discuss these questions with your student(s).
   a. When Paul went to a new city, where did he preach first?
   b. Why was Paul's education important?
   c. What were the Pharisees like?
   d. Can you give examples of Paul the persecutor?
   e. What do you know about Paul's conversion?
   f. What were the three convictions that motivated Paul?
   g. Why did the center for missionary activity shift from Jerusalem to Antioch?
2. Instruct the students on the different ways that a person can utilize the Bible in leading a person to the Lord. After ample preparation has been made, allow the students the opportunity to do an actual demonstration of leading one of their friends to the Lord.
3. Write and do a play of the time that Paul went before Festus and Felix and made the trip to Rome.
4. Assign each student a missions-type project in which they must complete an assigned task around their home church, with the pastor's approval; e.g., cleaning the bathrooms, mowing the lawn, straightening the hymn books; some sort of constructive type project that will give them a chance to show their idea of doing something for the Lord rather than just sitting. After they have completed this project, you should lead them in a meaningful discussion about service for the Lord.
5. Invite a missionary to speak about what it takes to become a missionary and the experiences he undergoes.
6. Write the account of your experience of being won to the Lord.
7. Record three interviews with three people from your church about how they were saved. Then write a report as to what you discovered.
8. Interview your pastor. Find out what type of preparations he had to make to become a pastor.
9. Interview your parents and find out what type of preparations they had to make to take on the responsibilities that they now assume. Write a report about your discoveries.

Section II – Paul's First Two Missionary Journeys

1. Discuss these questions with your student(s).
   a. After the conversion of Sergius Paulus, Paul was to be called by his Roman name. Why?
   b. Why did John Mark leave Paul and Barnabas?
   c. Why were Paul and Barnabas persecuted?
   d. What is a Judaizer?

     e. What things did James say that the Gentile believers should keep themselves from?
     f. Why did Paul and Barnabas not go together for the second missionary journey?
     g. Why were Paul and Silas jailed at Philippi?
     h. What subjects did Paul speak about to the Council on Mars Hill?

2. If your students have been working on soul winning, take them to a park for a ministry of witnessing.
3. Invite an ex-convict who has accepted the Lord to relate some of his or her "more relatable" stories to the class.
4. Invite a city prison official to come and talk to the class about present conditions within the city jails.
5. Discuss the evils of the occult.
6. Think back to the days of Paul and write a story about what it was like to witness back then.
7. Write a paragraph on how modern transportation has helped missionaries today.

Section III – Paul's Third Missionary Journey, Last Years, and Message
1. Discuss these questions with your student(s).
     a. For what reason did Paul leave Ephesus?
     b. How do you suppose Paul thought he was going to go to Rome?
     c. What false teaching entered the church at Colossae?
     d. How did Paul probably die?
     e. What are First Timothy and Titus about?
     f. What is Second Timothy about?
     g. Why did Paul write his letters?
     h. What was Paul's main emphasis in his teachings?
     i. What is the doctrine of man?
     j. What was Paul's view on the Law?
     k. What was Paul's view on the person and the work of Christ?
     l. What is the body of Christ?
2. Organize a field trip to a local missionary's work and ask him to take the student(s) with him on a typical day's work.
3. Break the class into three groups and have each section do a pictograph of one of the missionary journeys that Paul went on. Then display it for the parents at the next parent-teacher affair.
4. Write to a missionary and find out all that you can about him and his work.
5. Write a missionary story about yourself as a missionary undergoing a great deal of persecution.
6. Study further the lives of Silas and Barnabas. Write a report about your discoveries.

Materials Needed for LIFEPAC

Required: Suggested:
Bible

Additional Learning Activities

Section I – Preparing for Eternity

1. Discuss these questions with your student(s).
   a. When did eternity begin for the believer?
   b. What was the Roman road?
   c. What was the Sanhedrin?
   d. What does it mean to grow spiritually?
   e. How is a Christian ever a winner?
   f. What does it mean to lead a sacrificial life?
   g. What does it mean to live a separated life?
2. Name three blessings and give details about what they are.
3. Instruct students on leading an individual to Christ.
4. Practice on each other over a period of several days to lead someone to Christ. Ultimately have them work on it in front of the entire class.
5. Several students work together to make a poster dealing with eternity. Place the best ones on the bulletin board.
6. Make a listing of the blessings that God has given to you over the past few weeks. Share these with your teacher and have a short prayer session thanking God and asking Him for continued strength.
7. Select a witnessing target and begin witnessing to that person. Record the reactions that you received from your target and then write a report about it.

Section II – The Judgment Seat of Christ

1. Discuss these questions with your student(s).
   a. How do we know that Christ is the Judge of the living and the dead?
   b. What differences exist between a human judge and Christ?
   c. What is the purpose of the judgment seat of Christ?
   d. What motive should we use to do work for Christ?
   e. What happens to those Christians who stand empty-handed at the trying of fire?
   f. Can you name the different crowns and their purposes?
2. Write a play about the judgment seat of Christ. Have students take parts and read it aloud in class and then discuss it.
3. Ask your pastors what they believe that the judgment seat of Christ will be like. Some students lead in an open discussion about their discoveries.
4. Research how a judge makes a decision. Write your discoveries in a report and do a comparison of the human judge to Christ and how He will judge.
5. Ask your teacher about a service project that he might suggest that you could perform for your church. Then write a report as to how you felt performing the service.

Section III – The Great White Throne Judgment

1. Discuss the purpose of the judgment of unbelievers.
2. Describe the great white throne judgment.
3. Discuss what will happen to those who are never saved.
4. Describe hell.
5. Make a play like the old radio program "The War of the Worlds." Read the account of people's reactions to this classic produced by Orson Welles. Compare to what the Rapture will be like and also the great white throne judgment.
6. Draw or paint your idea of the two judgments that will be taking place.
7. Write a story about a dream that you had and how God allowed you to peek into hell and to see what it was like. Then describe it.
8. Do a comparison chart of the great white throne judgment and the eternity without God. Show all similarities and differences and then write your findings in a report.

Materials Needed for LIFEPAC

Required: Suggested:
Bible   None

Additional Learning Activities

Section I – God: The Source of All Authority

1. Discuss these questions with your class.
    a. What rights did God have as the Creator?
    b. What are natural laws?
    c. What are some of the instincts of different types of animals?
    d. What are the divine laws?
    e. What limitations might Jesus have felt as a man?
    f. Whose lives and words make up the New Testament?
    g. What is the work of the Holy Spirit?
    h. According to the Lord, which is the greatest commandment?

2. Using construction paper, make the two tablets containing the Ten Commandments and write them in. Out of a second set of construction paper, make another two tablets and write in Mom and Dad's ten commandments.

3. Write a poem about loving God with all of your heart, soul, strength, and mind.

4. Make a list of the days of Creation and record what God created on that day. Then, choose one of those days and write a report as to how God holds that aspect of creation together and what it would be like if He did not hold it together.

5. Students may write stories about a time when they did not overcome temptation and then a second story when they were able to overcome it with God's help. The students may then share their stories with the class.

Section II – Authority in the Family

1. Discuss responsibilities that parents give to their children.

2. Discuss Judges 17:6 and the fact that today's families often do not follow God's plan for authority. What have been the consequences for our society due to this unfortunate fact?

3. Discuss what it means to honor your parents. What are some practical ways in which this can be done? Pray with your students that they might learn to do this better.

4. Divide the class (or family) into two teams in order to debate this question: "Why should parents spank their children?" Search the Scriptures to see what God says about parental discipline of children.

5. Make up and present a play in which children have authority over parents. Discuss the consequences of such a situation.

6. Make a list of the responsibilities that you have at home. Write a short report as to how you would change any or all of your responsibilities to give yourself either more or less and tell why you would make the change.

7. Write a short story about the best day that you ever had with your family.

Section III – Government: Agent of Authority and Law

1. Discuss these questions with your class.
   a. Why is government necessary?
   b. Why is it good to delegate responsibility?
   c. What was the difference between a society ruled by a king and a society ruled by a judge?
   d. Why is it difficult for an absolute monarchy to be efficient?
   e. What are the pros and cons to each of the different types of government presented in this LIFEPAC?
   f. Why should Christians take an active part in the government of their country?

2. Invite a policeman to come and talk to the students about people who do not want to listen to the authority over them.

3. Take a field trip to a local legislative meeting and observe government in action.

4. The students may discuss the responsibilities that they have as citizens of this country.

5. Make a chart showing how democracy is run and a second chart showing how a different form of government is run. Write a report telling which one you would rather live under and why.

6. Write a story as to what it would be like if the freedoms of religion and speech were taken away from the American people.

Materials Needed for LIFEPAC

Required: Suggested:
Bible   None

Additional Learning Activities

Section I – God and His Angels

1. Break into groups for a class Scripture search on the subject of angels. Find out as much as possible. Pool all the information for a class presentation.

2. Choose a leader for a discussion concerning the presence of God. Make it plain that the Lord is with a person at all times and He knows everything that a person thinks and does.

3. Do a research project about how God's presence can help you. Use more detail than has already been mentioned in this LIFEPAC. In your report, discuss God's presence physically, mentally, and spiritually, and use personal examples to give further insight into your findings.

4. Have the students write stories about their guardian angels and how they think they have been helped by them. Allow the students to share their stories with the class.

Section II – The Bible: God's Word

1. Show a video or film about the theory of evolution, and discuss how it contradicts the Word of God. Help the students identify false assumptions about the theory as shown in the film.

2. Write a play about the trial, Crucifixion, and Resurrection of the Lord. Students can perform the play as a production for their parents.

3. Choose a leader for a class discussion on what it would have been like had the Lord not risen.

4. Do a pictograph or class mural of the trial, death, and Resurrection of the Lord.

5. Make a class chart showing the correct order of the books of the Bible. After each book, list who wrote it and the year in which it was written. Be creative in decorating your chart, and display it in a prominent place in the classroom.

Section III – Living for God (Part One)

1. Discuss these questions with your class.
   a. How was God faithful to Abraham?
   b. What is obedience?
   c. How were David and Jonah obedient?
   d. How were Paul and John good examples of loving service to God?

2. Prepare a poster or mural on the fruit of the Spirit.

3. Each student may choose an area of research on service for the Lord. Present your findings in a two-and-a-half to three-and-a-half-minute speech.

4. As a class activity develop a film on God's "Hall of Faith." Act out the stories of how these people got there.

5. Make out a goal chart for yourself in areas where you can be faithful on a daily basis. Record your faithfulness and unfaithfulness, then see how well you met your standards. Write a report as to what you discover and turn it in to your teacher.

6. Do a pictograph of Paul's journeys to Damascus.

Section IV – Living for God (Part Two)

1. Discuss these questions with your class.
    a. What is God's chain of command for home authority?
    b. What is the difference between natural laws and divine laws?
    c. What are the three duties of a Christian at home?
    d. What are some of the duties of a Christian at school?
    e. What are some of the duties of a Christian at work?
    f. What are some of the benefits and disadvantages of eternity?
2. Make a listing on the board of the student's suggestions concerning what a Christian's example is to be at school, at home, and at church. Create a chart or poster from the list.
3. Go to your pastor and ask him for an organizational and chain-of-command chart for your church. Make the chart out yourself and then turn it in to your teacher.
4. Ask your parents for a list of jobs that you could complete around the home for them without pay. Put these jobs into a daily listing and complete them without having to be told. Then write a report about what you had to do and how you felt about it.

TESTS & KEYS

Reproducible Tests
for use with the Bible 500
Teacher's Guide

Name _____

Write *true* **or** *false* (each answer, 2 points).

1. _____ The Scriptures say that those who lived in Old Testament times were pleasing to God because of the good deeds they did.

2. _____ David was born in Bethlehem.

3. _____ When King Saul was killed in battle, David mourned him.

4. _____ John was probably the youngest of the apostles.

5. _____ Paul mostly preached in small, remote villages.

6. _____ At the Cross, Jesus entrusted Mary to Peter.

7. _____ Noah lived among ungodly people.

8. _____ Ruth was a native of Moab.

9. _____ Stephen was the first Christian martyr.

10. _____ Abraham is only honored by Christians.

Write the correct answer in each blank (each answer, 4 points).

11. The apostle _____ wrote that believers are laborers together with God.

12. _____ was called "a man after God's own heart."

13. Turning back to the Lord after sinning is called _____ .

14. David spared the life of King _____ .

15. Abraham was known for his _____ .

16. Peter died as a _____ for his faith.

17. The Christian should keep his eyes on _____ .

18. As soon as Abraham arrived in Canaan, he built a(n) _____ .

19. God's _____ toward Nineveh made Jonah unhappy.

20. Paul was a _____ when he preached in Rome.

Match these items (each answer, 2 points).

21. _____	Canaan	a.	house of God
22. _____	co-laborer	b.	almost sacrificed
23. _____	Lot	c.	land promised to Abraham
24. _____	Paul's trade	d.	tentmaking
25. _____	Peter's trade	e.	to work with God
26. _____	Bethel	f.	anointed David king
27. _____	Gamaliel	g.	Paul's teacher
28. _____	John	h.	Abraham's nephew
29. _____	Samuel	i.	fisherman
30. _____	Isaac	j.	Apostle of love

Write the letter of the correct answer on each line (each answer, 2 points).

31. Naomi was Ruth's _____ .
    a. mother-in-law   b. sister   c. daughter

32. Hannah's _____ is one of the most beautiful in the Bible.
    a. dress   b. home   c. prayer

33. _____ led the first Passover.
    a. Enoch   b. Moses   c. Jesus

34. God promised Abraham that his _____ would be numerous.
    a. sheep   b. descendants   c. friends

35. _____ was exiled for his faith in Jesus.
    a. Andrew   b. David   c. John

Answer these questions (each answer, 5 points).

36. What is faith? _____

    _____

    _____

37. Why is the Christian life pictured as a race in Hebrews, chapter 12?_____

    _____

    _____

Date _____

Score _____

Possible Score _____ **100** _____

Name _____

Write the correct answer in each blank (each answer, 3 points).

1. The angel _____ is mentioned in both the Old and New Testaments.

2. _____ was sent to destroy the works of Satan.

3. _____ are personal beings and have intelligence and free wills.

4. An angel prevented _____ from sacrificing his son, Isaac.

5. An angel protected _____ from lions.

6. God wants us to cast all our _____ on Him.

7. The angel said that John the Baptist would be a _____ .

8. The angel said that Jesus would be the _____ .

9. Twelve _____ of angels were ready to help Jesus when He was arrested by the mob.

10. God created everything that exists, both visible and _____ .

Match these items (each answer, 2 points).

11. _____ angel   a. has no body or material

12. _____ Michael   b. wrestled an angel

13. _____ evil spirit   c. met an angel in the burning bush

14. _____ spirit   d. messenger

15. _____ kinds of dangers   e. sinned and rebelled

16. _____ a Christian's enemy   f. met an angel in Samaria

17. _____ Jacob   g. physical, spiritual

18. _____ Gabriel   h. the devil

19. _____ Philip   i. appeared to Mary

20. _____ Moses   j. archangel in Bible

Write *true* **or** *false* (each answer, 2 points).

21. _____ Some angels have a body and a spirit.

22. _____ Angels have different rank and authority.

23. _____ Only prayer and fasting can help Christians overcome the powers of darkness.

24. _____ Angels are extremely swift.

25. _____ Something can be real even though you do not see it.

26. _____ Jacob had several experiences with angels.

27. _____ God spoke to Moses face to face and told Moses who He was.

28. _____ Angels do not get sick or tired, nor do they need any sleep.

29. _____ The Bible calls the devil our "adversary."

30. _____ Two angels appeared to Lot and told him to stay in Sodom.

31. _____ Jesus needed protection and guidance from angels.

32. _____ Angels are not to be worshiped.

33. _____ An angel told Joseph to flee to Egypt.

34. _____ Only one angel appeared to the shepherds.

35. _____ Gabriel made an announcement to Mary.

Answer these questions (each answer, 5 points).

36. What are some things that angels do that show they are personal beings?

   _____

   _____

   _____

   _____

37. How can angels be real even though they are invisible? (Give examples).

   _____

   _____

   _____

   _____

38. When were 3 times that angels were involved during the public ministry of Jesus and at the end of His earthly ministry?

_____

_____

_____

_____

_____

39. Describe 3 appearances of angels in the early church after Jesus' earthly ministry recorded in the book of Acts.

_____

_____

_____

_____

_____

Date _____

Score _____

Possible Score _____100_____

Bible 503 Alternate Test

Name _____

Fill in the blank with the correct answer (each answer, 4 points).

1. A _____ is a person who gives advice or guidance.

2. A _____ is someone who works for God in telling the good news of salvation in Jesus Christ.

3. God is everywhere, and He is the _____ everywhere.

4. Regarding the attribute of truth, Jesus said, "I am _____ ."

5. God's knowledge is _____ .

6. Because God is faithful, He will keep His _____ .

7. Because God speaks, thinks, and loves, He is _____ .

8. _____ put out a fleece of wool on the ground to see if God's presence was really with him.

9. _____ became known as the great apostle to the North American Indians.

10. _____ was called "The Small Woman."

Write *true* **or** *false* (each answer, 2 points).

11. _____ God can hear everyone's prayers at the same time.

12. _____ When David Brainerd died, he lost the presence of God.

13. _____ David Livingstone was a missionary to India.

14. _____ Job always knew that the Lord heard him.

15. _____ Paul said that all our needs would be provided through Jesus Christ.

16. _____ God called David "a man after my own heart."

17. _____ God provides only spiritual things for us.

18. _____ God speaks to us only through the Bible.

19. _____ Because God is spirit, He has no body.

20. _____ Because God's faithfulness is everywhere, He will forgive sin anywhere if we ask Him.

Write the letter of the correct answer in the blank (each answer, 3 points).

21. God is _____ .
   a. personal   b. impersonal   c. a force

22. God will do _____ that He has promised.
    a. some things   b. everything   c. most things

23. According to the apostle John in his first letter, God is _____ .
    a. in heaven   b. love   c. here

24. God is not _____ anywhere in the universe.
    a. dwelling   b. present   c. absent

25. God listens to prayers _____ .
    a. one at a time   b. 2 or 3 together   c. all over the world at any time

26. _____ was a great missionary to Africa.
    a. David Brainerd   b. David Livingstone   c. David Hudson

27. Gladys Aylward was a missionary in _____ .
    a. China   b. Japan   c. Taiwan

28. _____ means everywhere present.
    a. omniscience   b. omnipotent   c. omnipresence

29. God is so near that He listens to us like a _____ .
    a. parent   b. doctor   c. teacher

30. David said that the source of his salvation was _____ .
    a. the Bible   b. himself   c. the Lord

Answer these questions (each answer, 5 points).

31.   What are 5 attributes of God that are present everywhere?
       a. _____
       b. _____
       c. _____
       d. _____
       e. _____

32.   What are 3 ways God speaks to us?
       a. _____
       b. _____
       c. _____

Date _____
Score _____
Possible Score _____ 100 _____

Bible 504 Alternate Test

Name _____

Match these items (each answer, 2 points).

1. _____ God's Word
2. _____ book of fulfillment
3. _____ author of the Bible
4. _____ main Bible theme
5. _____ Old Testament language
6. _____ New Testament language
7. _____ letters to churches
8. _____ writing material
9. _____ Matthew, Mark, Luke, John
10. _____ first Bible book

a. Epistles
b. Revelation
c. Romans
d. the Bible
e. the Gospels
f. Exodus
g. Genesis
h. God
i. Hebrew
j. papyrus
k. Greek
l. God's loving plan of salvation

Write *true* **or** *false* (each answer, 2 points).

11. _____ The Bible tells one continuous story.
12. _____ The Bible had over one hundred different writers.
13. _____ The main character of the Bible is Jesus Christ.
14. _____ The Bible is mainly a book of geography.
15. _____ The book of Psalms is the largest Bible book.
16. _____ Saul was God's choice as Israel's first king.
17. _____ It took more than one thousand years to write the Bible.
18. _____ The New Testament completes the Old Testament.
19. _____ Some of Paul's Epistles were written from prison.
20. _____ The church begins in the Gospel of John.

Write the letter of the correct answer on each line (each answer, 2 points).

21. The word *testament* means _____ .
    a. book   c. agreement
    b. sacrifice   d. history

22. The Protestant Bible has _____ books.
    a. twenty-seven   c. thirty-nine
    b. sixty-six   d. seventy-three

23. The book of Romans is a book of _____ .
    a. prophecy   c. poetry
    b. history   d. the Epistles

24. Israel was led into the Promised Land by _____ .
    a. Moses   c. Joshua
    b. David   d. Solomon

Write these verses from memory (each answer, 5 points).

25. Psalm 119:105 _____

    _____

    _____

26. John 3:16 _____

    _____

    _____

    _____

Complete these lists (each item, 3 points).

27.   List the two main divisions of the Bible.

       a. _____

       b. _____

28   List three of the Old Testament books of poetry

       a. _____

       b. _____

       c. _____

29. List one Old Testament book of prophecy and one New Testament book of prophecy.

       Old Testament   a. _____
       New Testament   b. _____

30. Name the Synoptic Gospels.

       a. _____

       b. _____

       c. _____

After each book, write *Old Testament* **or** *New Testament* (each answer, 2 points).

31. Judges _____

32. 2 Timothy _____

33. Song of Solomon _____

34. Joel _____

35. Jude _____

36. Psalms _____

Date _____
Score _____
Possible Score _____ **100** _____

Name _____

Match these items (each answer, 3 points).

1. _____ Proverbs
2. _____ love
3. _____ correction
4. _____ beginning of wisdom
5. _____ industrious
6. _____ church
7. _____ parents
8. _____ spiritual gifts
9. _____ meddle
10. _____ humility

a. most important aspect of one's life

b. family of God

c. mind others' business

d. opposite of lazy

e. responsible for teaching children

f. may be more than words

g. a book containing God's wisdom

h. fear of the Lord

i. opposite of pride

j. used to build up the church

Answer *true* **or** *false* (each answer, 2 points).

11. _____ A Christian should avoid non-Christians.

12. _____ A lie is only made through speech.

13. _____ Parents and children should listen to each other.

14. _____ The discipline of God and parents is a sign of love for children.

15. _____ Children must obey parents as long as they are children and living in the home.

16. _____ Only a few sayings in Proverbs deal with wisdom.

17. _____ Helping the poor is important to the Lord.

18. _____ Public squares and gateways were places of business in Bible days.

19. _____ Only some Christians, like pastors and ministers, are called to use spiritual gifts in the church.

20. _____ The first place for children to learn about God is in Sunday School at church.

21. _____ Jesus cares a lot about our relationships with other people.

Complete these statements (each answer, 3 points).

22. God wants you to live a _____ in this world.

23. _____ means knowing the best way to live, act, and speak.

24. Jesus said, "By this all men will know that ye are my disciples, if ye have _____ one for another."

25. Christians are called to "… _____ in the grace and knowledge of our Lord and Savior Jesus Christ" (2 Peter 3:18).

26. Proverbs 4:13 says, "Take fast hold of _____ ; let her not go: keep her; for she is thy life."

27. Failing to keep promises is a type of _____ .

28. A cheerful heart is good _____ .

29. A Christian should take victory _____ .

30. A Christian should take defeat _____ .

31. The Christian should _____ all of self to the Holy Spirit.

Complete this list (each item, 2 points).

32. List the four "worlds" of a Christian.

   a. _____

   b. _____

   c. _____

   d. _____

Write these Bible verses from memory (each answer, 5 points).

33. John 13:34 _____

_____

_____

_____

34. Proverbs 9:10 _____

_____

_____

_____

Date _____
Score _____
Possible Score _____ **100** _____

Name _____

Match these items (each answer, 3 points).

1. _____ the Bible's oneness

2. _____ an enemy of the Bible

3. _____ predictions of the future

4. _____ God's "method" of Creation

5. _____ cannot be numbered

6. _____ shielded cosmic radiation

7. _____ carbon 14 dating

8. _____ a "god" of evolutionists

9. _____ belief or set of beliefs

10. _____ most practical evidence

a. doctrine

b. organic evolution

c. sanitation

d. assumes atmosphere remained the same

e. Christian experience

f. Diocletian

g. unity

h. chance

i. prophecy

j. the stars

k. His Word

l. water canopy

Answer *true* **or** *false* (each answer, 2 points).

11. _____ Jesus believed that the Old Testament was God's Word.

12. _____ The Bible was written by about twenty-seven human writers.

13. _____ Some parts of the Bible do not agree with other parts.

14. _____ God's Word is imperishable.

15. _____ Christians believe that God created everything that exists.

16. _____ People can get a glimpse of God's glory through what He has created in the heavens.

17. _____ The theory of evolution is one way that man can deny his need for a Savior.

18. _____ There is no proof for the theory of evolution.

19. _____ The church began publicly of the day of Pentecost.

20. _____ Jesus' predictions that He would rise from the dead are recorded in the four Gospels.

Bible 506 Alternate Test

Complete these lists (each item, 3 points).

21. List three doctrines of the Christian faith that are being particularly challenged today.

    a. _____

    b. _____

    c. _____

22. List three pieces of evidence from history that show the Bible is God's Word.

    a. _____

    b. _____

    c. _____

23. List four false assumptions in the theory of evolution.

    a. _____
      _____

    b. _____
      _____

    c. _____
      _____

    d. _____
      _____

Complete these statements (each answer, 3 points).

24. The word _____ means the direct influence of God on the human writers of the Bible.

25. David wrote that the firmament (the sky above us) showed God's _____ .

26. The Law told the Israelites not to eat or even touch certain things because they were considered _____ .

27. The Resurrection of Jesus is a _____ event.

28. The Old Testament _____ that Christ would rise from the dead.

Write this Bible verse from memory (this answer, 5 points).

29. Hebrews 4:12 _____

    _____

    _____

    _____

Date _____

Score _____

Possible Score _____ 100 _____

Name _____

Match these items (each answer, 2 points).

1. _____ Silas
2. _____ Barnabas
3. _____ Gamaliel
4. _____ Sergius Paulus
5. _____ Philippi
6. _____ Cyprus
7. _____ Mars Hill
8. _____ Corinth
9. _____ synagogues
10. _____ Demetrius

a. Paul's first Gentile convert
b. silversmith in Ephesus, led riot against Paul
c. location where Paul spoke to the Greek council
d. Paul was taught by him
e. partner on second and third journey
f. Paul's favorite church was here
g. two letters were sent here
h. an island south of Asia Minor
i. partner on first missionary journey
j. where the Jews worshiped
k. the emperor of Rome
l. Paul spent three years here

Write *true* **or** *false* (each answer, 2 points).

11. _____ Paul was a Jew and a Roman citizen by birth.
12. _____ Philippians, Colossians, Hebrews, and Luke were all written by Paul.
13. _____ Luke wrote Acts.
14. _____ Paul was a missionary to the Gentiles.
15. _____ Paul never preached in the synagogues.

Answer these questions with complete sentences (each answer, 5 points).

16. Where did Paul spend the last years of his life? _____

_____

17. How can we live a Christian life today? _____

_____

Complete these items (each answer, 10 points).

18. Trace Paul's second missionary journey.

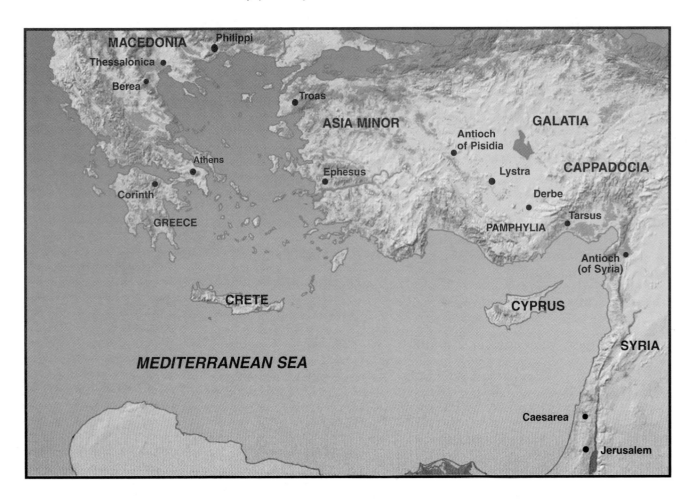

19. Trace Paul's trip to Rome

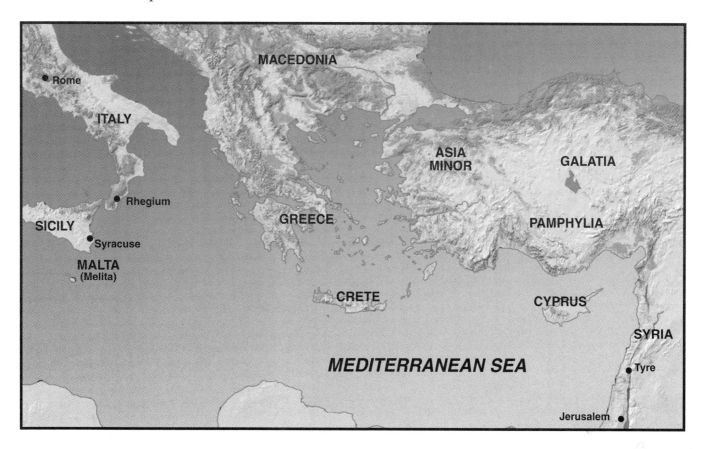

Write the letter of the correct answer in the blank (each answer, 2 points).

20. The letter that was not written from Rome was _____ .
    a. Colossians   c. Ephesians
    b. Philippians   d. Galatians

21. For three years Paul was at the church _____ .
    a. Philippi   c. Corinth
    b. Ephesus   d. Antioch

22. Paul had a vision to "come over into _____ ."
    a. Achaia   c. Macedonia
    b. Cilicia   d. Syria

23. The main part of Paul's message is salvation by _____ .
    a. the Law   c. fighting heresies
    b. Christ in you   d. none of these

24. The letters to the Thessalonians were mostly about _____ .
    a. the Second Coming   c. heresies in Judaism
    b. church membership   d. the Jerusalem Council

Complete these statements (each answer, 3 points).

25. Paul was taught the skill of _____ .

26. Paul studied to become a Jewish _____ .

27. Paul's _____ was on the road to Damascus.

28. Paul taught for _____ year(s) in Antioch of Syria.

29. Antioch of Pisidia was on the mainland of _____ .

30. After the first missionary journey, Paul went to the _____ Council.

31. Paul's partner on the first missionary journey was _____ .

32. In Philippi, Paul led a lady to Jesus Christ named _____ .

33. Two important towns in Achaia are Corinth and _____ .

34. Paul was greatly helped by Aquila and _____ .

Date _____
Score _____
Possible Score _____ **100** _____

Match these items (each answer, 2 points).

1. _____ unsaved
2. _____ Bema
3. _____ conscience
4. _____ Jesus
5. _____ Patmos
6. _____ all have sinned
7. _____ Paul
8. _____ love for God
9. _____ for soul winners
10. _____ for those who love Christ's appearing

a. where John saw the vision
b. rewards
c. judge of living and dead
d. crown of rejoicing
e. crown of righteousness
f. great white throne judgment
g. glory
h. knowledge of right and wrong
i. motive for service
j. content
k. Romans 3:23

Complete these statements (each answer, 3 points).

11. Everyone has a _____ that will last forever.

12. God loved the _____ and, therefore, gave His Son.

13. The foundation for our Christian life is _____ .

14. The man who knew that Jesus was a teacher sent from God was _____ .

15. When a person dies without ever receiving Christ, he will receive_____ destruction.

16. Crowns are heavenly _____ .

17. Tears of sorrow and pain will be shed by residents of _____ .

18. The biggest drawback to spiritual growth is _____ .

19. If a man wants to see the kingdom of God, he must be _____ _____ .

20. The most lasting work that can be done for God is leading someone to _____ .

Write *true* **or** *false* (each answer, 2 points).

21. _____ Nothing can separate us from the love of God.

22. _____ An athlete must train his mind and body if he wants to win.

23. _____ Running the Christian race with perfection is God's desire for us.

24. _____ Hell is totally detailed so that scholars already know what it is like.

25. _____ Our work will be judged by the blowing of the wind.

26. _____ Christians will be judged so that others can see how good they were.

27. _____ Eternity without God is darkness and torment.

28. _____ God has appointed angels to be our judge.

29. _____ It is possible to have joy in your heart even though you feel unhappy.

Answer these questions (each answer, 5 points).

30. Eternity for the unsaved is described vividly in the Bible. Tell what you think it will be like for the unbeliever in his final torment.

_____

_____

_____

31. Name and describe four of the crowns mentioned in the Bible.

   a. _____

   b. _____

   c. _____

   d. _____

Write the letter of the correct answer on each line (each answer, 2 points).

32. A pastor's responsibilities do not include _____ .
   a. feeding the flock   b. setting an example   c. telling everyone what to do

33. Your flesh wrestles against your _____ .
   a. spirit   b. growth   c. sin

34. This person is responsible for the choices you make. _____
   a. mother   b. you   c. father

35. The Holy Spirit gives the believer _____ .
   a. joy   b. sin   c. flesh

36. How many of God's blessings are good? _____
   a. none   b. some   c. all

37. They gave alms for their own glory. _____
   a. Sadducees   b. hypocrites   c. Jews

38. When the storm came up from the Sea of Galilee, Jesus was _____ .
   a. preaching   b. sleeping   c. witnessing

39. Jesus and Nicodemus met together in the _____ .
    a. morning   b. afternoon   c. evening

40. Nicodemus was an elder of the _____ .
    a. Sadducees   b. Sanhedrin   c. Pharisees

41. To illustrate works that would be burned, Paul used hay, stubble, and _____ .
    a. wood   b. gold   c. brush

42. God is perfect and _____ .
    a. just   b. whole   c. good

Date _____
Score _____
Possible Score _____ 100 _____

Bible 509 Alternate Test

Name _____

Fill in the blank with the correct answer (each answer, 4 points).

1. According to Genesis, men and women were to rule the earth with love and under obedience to _____ .

2. _____ law is God's eternal law for human beings.

3. Before He ascended into heaven, Jesus promised that He and the Father would send the _____.

4. The _____ is the center of authority that God delegated to human beings when He created them.

5. _____ delegate authority to children according to their age and ability.

6. _____ is a model of obedience for all Christians.

7. God revealed His supernatural laws in the _____ .

8. _____ became the leader of the Israelites when Moses died.

9. Jesus was born into a devout _____ family.

10. A democracy is a government in which the _____ choose the government leaders.

Write *true* **or** *false* (each answer, 2 points).

11. _____ God created woman first, then man.

12. _____ God blessed both Adam and Eve.

13. _____ A child has the right to decide whether or not he will accept his parents' decisions.

14. _____ All creation is governed by God's authority.

15. _____ The Holy Spirit is the Counselor who guides Christians.

16. _____ As a young boy, Jesus was sometimes disobedient to His parents.

17. _____ Some authority in heaven and on earth has been given to Jesus.

18. _____ Saul was the last and greatest of the judges.

19. _____ Moses was given the Ten Commandments by God.

20. _____ Abraham was a democratic leader.

Write the letter of the correct answer on the line (each answer, 3 points).

21. _____ were our first parents.
    a. Abraham & Sarah   b. Adam & Eve   c. Elkanah & Hannah

22. The _____ is the pastor of the family.
    a. oldest son   b. mother   c. father

23. Some time alone is a need of _____ .
    a. parents   b. children   c. parents & children

24. The greatest _____ is to love God.
    a. commandment   b. teaching   c. service

25. The Scriptures are the _____ authority of God.
    a. written   b. spoken   c. delegated

26. The form of government practiced by Abraham was _____ .
    a. democratic   b. patriarchal   c. Mosaic

27. When all the power of a government rests with the king, it is called a(n) _____ .
    a. absolute monarchy   b. republic   c. limited monarchy

28. _____ is a good Biblical example of someone who was obedient and helpful to his parents.
    a. King Saul   b. Judas   c. David

29. The _____ tells us to love God and our neighbor.
    a. golden rule   b. law of love   c. Lord's prayer

30. Parents are more ready to _____ a child who respects their standards.
    a. trust   b. train   c. discipline

Answer these questions (each answer, 5 points).

31. How does the Holy Spirit help a Christian? _____

    _____

    _____

    _____

    _____

32. What are three reasons for the need of government, and what would happen if there was no government?
    a. _____
    b. _____
    c. _____
    d. _____

Date _____

Score _____

Possible Score _____ 100 _____

Bible 510 Alternate Test

Name _____

Match these items (each answer, 3 points).

1. _____ Philip

2. _____ Daniel

3. _____ Elisha

4. _____ theme of the Bible

5. _____ author(s) of Bible

6. _____ angel

7. _____ John

8. _____ Paul

9. _____ David

10. _____ Jesus

a. God

b. once persecuted Christians

c. came to give us eternal life

d. one continuous story

e. was led by an angel to tell an Ethiopian about Jesus

f. forty-one writers

g. the disciple whom Jesus loved

h. musician, shepherd, and king

i. was protected by an angel in a lions' den

j. God's loving plan of salvation

k. an army of angels protected him from the Syrians

l. messenger of God

Answer *true* **or** *false* (each answer, 2 points).

11. _____ There are some places where we can hide from the presence of God.

12. _____ Angels can quickly travel from heaven to earth.

13. _____ The Bible has two main sections.

14. _____ The shortest part of the Old Testament is history.

15. _____ Knowledge of the Resurrection changes people's lives.

16. _____ Both the Old and New Testaments contain parts of history and epistles.

17. _____ The Bible has scientific truth in it.

18. _____ Paul was a missionary to the Gentiles.

19. _____ God has the rights of a creator for His authority.

20. _____ Receiving correction is always easy.

Complete these statements (each answer, 3 points).

21. You can walk and talk with God because He is a _____ God.

22. Angels are _____ spirits, sent forth to minister for them who shall be heirs of salvation.

23. The theory of _____ says that the complexity of the DNA molecule had to have an intelligent designer.

24. Hebrews, chapter 11 is sometimes called the "Hall of _____."

25. A Christian worker is called to be _____ and industrious.

Write the letter of the correct answer in the blank (each answer, 2 points).

26. An early form of government of Old Testament people was _____ .
    a. patriarchal   b. tribal   c. kingdom   d. a, b, and c

27. People should serve God because they _____ Him
    a. fear   b. love   c. respect   d. love

28. David was a man after God's own _____ .
    a. will   b. power   c. heart   d. knowledge

29. The New Testament has _____ main parts.
    a. two   b. three   c. four   d. five

30. God made all things in heaven and earth, both visible and _____ .
    a. personal   b. material   c. far away   d. invisible

List these items (each listed item, 3 points).

31. List three beliefs of Christian doctrine that are particularly challenged today.
    a. _____
    b. _____
    c. _____

32. List any two duties of children at home.
    a. _____
    b. _____

Answer this question (this answer, 5 points).

33. What are some reasons that the Bible can be considered as one complete book?

    _____
    _____
    _____
    _____
    _____
    _____
    _____
    _____

Write this Scripture verse from memory (this answer, 5 points).

34. John 3:16 _____

_____

_____

_____

_____

_____

_____

_____

Date _____
Score _____
Possible Score _____ 100 _____

1. false
2. true
3. true
4. true
5. false
6. false
7. true
8. true
9. true
10. false
11. Paul
12. David
13. repentance
14. Saul
15. faith
16. martyr
17. Christ
18. altar
19. mercy
20. prisoner
21. c
22. e
23. h
24. d
25. i
26. a
27. g
28. j
29. f
30. b
31. a
32. c
33. b
34. b
35. c
36. Faith is the substance of things hoped for, the evidence of things not seen.
37. Christians are encouraged to serve God faithfully. If we take our eyes off Jesus, we may lose the race. The goal of the race is Jesus.

1. Gabriel

2. Jesus

3. Angels

4. Abraham

5. Daniel

6. cares

7. forerunner

8. Messiah

9. legions

10. invisible

11. d

12. j

13. e

14. a

15. g

16. h

17. b

18. i

19. f

20. c

21. false

22. true

23. false

24. true

25. true

26. true

27. false

28. true

29. true

30. false

31. false

32. true

33. true

34. false

35. true

36. Angels think, sing, obey, plan, and show emotions. They are wise, can make choices, and can speak to people.

37. Just as the wind and electricity are real, even though we can't see them, so angels are real.

38. Any 3:
   1. The angels waited on and strengthened Jesus after He was tempted by Satan in the desert.
   2. Jesus was strengthened by an angel in the Garden of Gethsemane.
   3. An angel rolled back the stone at Jesus' tomb and informed the two women that Jesus had risen.
   4. Angels accompanied Jesus at His Ascension into Heaven.
   5. After Jesus' Ascension, two angels spoke to Jesus' disciples about the Ascension and Jesus' second coming.

39. Suggested answers:
   1. An angel freed Peter from prison.
   2. An angel protected Paul and the sailors during a storm at sea.
   3. An angel led Philip to the Ethiopian who accepted Jesus and was baptized.

1. counselor
2. missionary
3. same
4. the truth
5. everywhere
6. promises
7. personal
8. Gideon
9. David Brainerd
10. Gladys Aylward
11. true
12. false
13. false
14. false
15. true
16. true
17. false
18. false
19. true
20. true
21. a
22. b
23. b
24. c
25. c
26. b
27. a

28. c
29. a
30. c
31. Any 5 – any order:
love, faithfulness, knowledge, truth, power, holiness, goodness
32. Any order:
a. through the Bible
b. through conscience
c. through the Holy Spirit

1. d

2. b

3. h

4. l

5. i

6. k

7. a

8. j

9. e

10. g

11. true

12. false

13. true

14. false

15. true

16. false

17. true

18. true

19. true

20. false

21. c

22. b

23. d

24. c

25. Thy word is a lamp unto my feet, and a light unto my path.

26. For God so loved the world, that he gave his only begotten Son, that whosoever believeth in him should not perish, but have everlasting life.

27. Either order:
    a. Old Testament
    b. New Testament

28. Any order:
    a. Job
    b. Psalms
    c. Proverbs
    or, Ecclesiastes, the Song of Solomon

29. a. Any of the Major or Minor Prophets of the Old Testament
    b. Revelation

30. Any order:
    a. Matthew
    b. Mark
    c. Luke

31. Old Testament

32. New Testament

33. Old Testament

34. Old Testament

35. New Testament

36. Old Testament

1. g
2. a
3. f
4. h
5. d
6. b
7. e
8. j
9. c
10. i
11. false
12. false
13. true
14. true
15. true
16. false
17. true
18. true
19. false
20. false
21. true
22. holy life
23. Wisdom
24. love
25. grow
26. instruction
27. lying

28. medicine
29. humbly
30. gracefully
31. yield
32. Any order:
    a. home
    b. church
    c. school
    d. work
33. A new commandment I give unto you, That ye love one another; as I have loved you, that ye also love one another.
34. The fear of the LORD is the beginning of wisdom: and the knowledge of the holy is understanding.

1. g

2. f

3. i

4. k

5. j

6. l

7. d

8. h

9. a

10. e

11. true

12. false

13. false

14. true

15. true

16. true

17. true

18. true

19. true

20. true

21. Any order:
a. The Bible as the Word of God
b. God's Creation of the world
c. The Resurrection of Jesus Christ

22. Any order:
a. the Bible's superiority
b. the Bible's popularity
c. the Bible's stability

23. Examples – any order:
a. They believe that the earth's atmosphere never changed.
b. They believe in an unknown first life organism.
c. They believe in the theory that life began in the ocean.
d. They believe that life evolved from simple life-form to the more complex.

24. inspiration

25. handiwork

26. unclean

27. historical

28. predicted

29. For the word of God is quick, and powerful, and sharper than any two-edged sword, piercing even to the dividing asunder of the soul and spirit, and of the joints and marrow, and is a discerner of the thoughts and intents of the heart.

1. e

2. i

3. d

4. a

5. f

6. h

7. c

8. g

9. j

10. b

11. true

12. false

13. true

14. true

15. false

16. He spent his last years in Rome. Much of that time was in prison.

17. We must let Christ live in us and let the Holy Spirit lead us.

18. (See page 84 for map and key.)

19. (See page 85 for map and key.)

20. d

21. b

22. c

23. b

24. a

25. tent-making

26. Pharisee

27. conversion

28. one

29. Asia Minor

30. Jerusalem

31. Barnabas

32. Lydia

33. Athens

34. Priscilla

18. Paul's Second Missionary Journey:

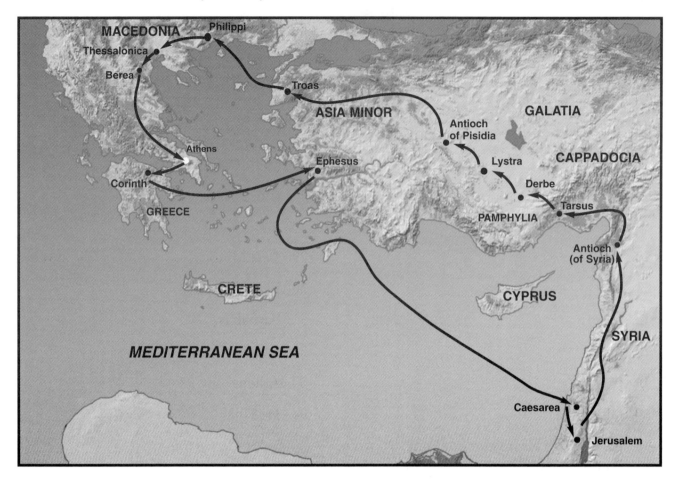

19. Paul's Journey to Rome:

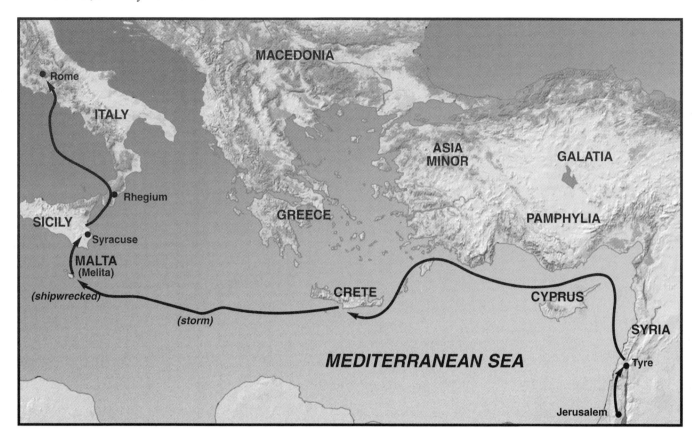

1. f
2. b
3. h
4. c
5. a
6. k
7. j
8. i
9. d
10. e
11. soul
12. world
13. Jesus
14. Nicodemus
15. everlasting
16. rewards
17. hell
18. sin
19. born again
20. Christ
21. true
22. true
23. false
24. false
25. false
26. false
27. true

28. false
29. true
30. Example:
There will be darkness, weeping, and gnashing of teeth. God and Jesus will not be there, so the residents of hell will spend eternity without love, joy, and peace.
31. Any order:
a. the crown of life – for those who love God and endure temptation
b. the crown of glory – for faithful ministers
c. the crown of rejoicing – for soul winners
d. the crown of righteousness – for those who love Christ's appearing
32. c
33. a
34. b
35. a
36. c
37. b
38. b
39. c
40. b
41. a
42. a

1. God

2. Divine

3. Holy Spirit

4. family

5. Parents

6. Jesus

7. Bible

8. Joshua

9. Jewish

10. people

11. false

12. true

13. false

14. true

15. true

16. false

17. false

18. false

19. true

20. false

21. b

22. c

23. c

24. a

25. a

26. b

27. a

28. c

29. b

30. a

31. Example: The Holy Spirit strengthens us inwardly. He helps us to live the law of love and to live God's will, even when it is difficult.

32. Governments are needed for:
    a. order
    b. safety
    c. the protection of rights.
    d. Chaos, confusion, and anxiety would result if there were no government.

1. e

2. i

3. k

4. j

5. f, a (either answer, or both answers)

6. l

7. g

8. b

9. h

10. c

11. false

12. true

13. true

14. false

15. true

16. false

17. true

18. true

19. true

20. false

21. personal

22. ministering

23. Intelligent Design

24. Faith

25. honest

26. a

27. b

28. c

29. a

30. d

31. Any order:
    a. the Bible as the Word of God
    b. God's Creation of the world
    c. the Resurrection of Jesus Christ

32. Any two, any order:
    a. love others
    b. hear and obey instruction
    c. receive correction
    d. learn correct behavior

33. Example (at least these four points should be mentioned):
    It has one main and true author: God.
    It has one main theme: God's loving plan of salvation.
    It has one main character: Jesus Christ.
    It has one purpose: to reveal the Word of God and the plan of salvation to man.

34. For God so loved the world, that he gave his only begotten Son, that whosoever believeth in him should not perish, but have everlasting life.

ANSWER KEYS

SECTION ONE

1.1   true

1.2   false

1.3   true

1.4   true

1.5   true

1.6   A believer has faith in God. He trusts, loves, and obeys God.

1.7   **Hebrews 11:1** – Now faith is the substance of things hoped for, the evidence of things not seen.

1.8   Any order:
a. Moslems
b. Jews
c. Christians

1.9   friend

1.10   75

1.11   Examples:
a. well-known
b. a blessing to the whole world

1.12   a. powerful
b. wicked nations

1.13   a. altar
b. sacrifices
c. the Lord's name (*or* God)

1.14   fellow-laborer

1.15   Example: Abraham told Lot to divide the land between them and separate.

1.16   Example: Lot chose the best and most fertile land, but it was located in the most wicked part of the country.

1.17   Example: Abraham's faith was strong, unshakable, and unwavering.

1.18   false

1.19   true

1.20   true

1.21   true

1.22   Adult check – possible answers:
Setting: The grazing lands of Abraham and Lot. The grazing lands divided and Lot settling along the Jordan River.

What God Did or Said: God told Abraham that lands in all directions would belong to Abraham and his descendants.
What Abraham Did or Said: Abraham believed God even though he could not understand. Abraham believed God could do anything He promised to do.
Abraham's Lesson to Us: We are to believe God's promises to us and have faith so strong that we keep praising God.

1.23   Adult check – possible answers:
Setting: A mountain top
What God Did or Said: God told Abraham to take his only son Isaac to a mountain and offer Isaac as a burnt sacrifice.
What Abraham Did or Said: Abraham immediately began to carry out God's request. Abraham proved his faith in God.
Abraham's Lesson to Us: Abraham showed us how to believe God's promises. He served God by proving to the world that God keeps His promises if we trust Him to do what He says in His Word.

1.24   Adult check – Examples: courageous, faithful, generous, kind, leader, obedient, prayerful, trusting

1.25   Any three: talented, handsome, strong, brave

1.26   his faith that the Lord was with him

1.27   a. bodyguard
b. harp

1.28 Example: David loved God very much and wanted to please God in all that he did.

1.29 Example: It proved that David had gained the victory over Goliath by the power of the Lord God.

1.30 David was made commander of Saul's army.

1.31 Saul felt jealous.

1.32 Jonathan helped David escape.

1.33 David called King Saul "the Lord's anointed."

1.34 He mourned their deaths by writing a song of mourning.

1.35 Any order:
a. Judah and Israel were united as one kingdom.
b. God's enemies were conquered and Israel had peace.
c. The nation prospered and people put God at the center of their lives.

1.36 Example: David sinned, as all people do, but he was quick to turn back to the Lord and ask for forgiveness and mercy.

1.37 heart

1.38 trusting

1.39 repentant *or* broken, contrite

1.40 worshipful

1.41 obedient *or* teachable

1.42 Adult check – possible answers:
Setting: A battleground in Judah. Israelites fighting against the Philistines.
What God Did or Said: When Samuel anointed David, the Spirit of the Lord came upon David in power. God helped David overcome Goliath, just as He had helped him overcome a bear and a lion in the past.

What David Did or Said: David boldly declared that since the Lord had delivered him from bears and lions, He would deliver him from Goliath. David also said that it was not by sword or spear that the Lord saves, because the battle is the Lord's.
David's Lesson to Us: God wants us to have strong faith and trust in Him.

1.43 Adult check – possible answers:
Setting: The countryside of Israel. In a cave.
What God Did or Said: God protected David and did not allow his enemies to harm or kill him.
What David Did or Said: Even though Saul was now trying to kill him, David would not kill or harm him because he respected Saul as "the Lord's anointed."
David's Lesson to Us: We should entrust our lives fully to the Lord and not try to seek revenge on those who have harmed us. God will be our vindication, because He knows who is right. God will protect us.

1.44 Adult check – possible answers:
Setting: David's heart
What God Did or Said: God punished David for his sins.
What David Did or Said: David humbly asked the Lord to wash away his iniquity and cleanse him from his sin. David had faith that God would forgive and restore him.
David's Lesson to Us: When we sin, we should be quick to ask forgiveness. We should repent in humility and have faith that God will forgive us and restore us to a right relationship with Him.

1.45 Adult check – examples: brave, handsome, strong, talented, trusting, obedient, repenting, humble, worshipful

SECTION TWO

2.1 Jesus Christ *or* the Lord

2.2 Any four: student, thinker, Christian, writer, teacher, missionary, man of prayer

2.3 Examples – any order:
a. He knew and loved the Scriptures.
b. He was familiar with people from every class and race.
c. He learned about different customs.
d. He learned different languages.

2.4 2, 5, 1, 6, 3, 4

2.5 Example: In persecuting those who loved and followed Jesus, it was as if Paul were persecuting Jesus himself.

2.6 Christ, and to die is gain

2.7 Christ

2.8 Christ

2.9 Example: In one city, Paul was stoned as Stephen had been stoned before. The people thought Paul was dead and dragged him from the city. Christians gathered around him and prayed. Paul recovered and went back into the city and continued to preach about Jesus.

2.10 "Believe on the Lord Jesus Christ, and thou shalt be saved...."

2.11 Example: The only thing that mattered to Paul was being faithful to the ministry Jesus had given him and to finish his life with joy.

2.12 a. Jerusalem
b. Caesarea
c. Sidon
d. Myra
e. Cnidus
f. Salmone
g. Lasea
h. Clauda
i. Malta
j. Syracuse
k. Rhegium
l. Puteoli
m. Three Taverns
n. Rome

2.13 Adult check – possible answers:
Setting: On the road to Damascus, a bright light from heaven shone upon Saul (Paul).
What God Did or Said: God said, "Saul, Saul, why are you persecuting me?"
What Paul Did or Said: Paul gave his heart to Christ. He asked, "Lord, what do you want me to do?" He spent every day after that serving Christ.
Paul's Lesson to Us: When the Lord is telling us something, we must obey quickly.

2.14 Adult check – possible answers:
Setting: Many cities
What God Did or Said: God sent Paul on his missionary journeys and guided him along the way.
What Paul Did or Said: Paul faithfully preached the good news about Jesus, witnessed to others about his faith in Jesus, baptized new converts, healed people through the power of the Holy Spirit, and wrote letters to various churches.
Paul's Lesson to Us: In spite of dangers, our main responsibility is to be true and loyal to God. We are to put God first. God will take care of us always.

2.15 Adult check – possible answers: courageous, faithful, helpful, leader, loyal, obedient, persevering, prayerful, trusting, zealous

2.16 Examples: John loved Jesus deeply and knew that Jesus had a deep love for him. When John wrote his Gospel, he referred to himself as "the disciple whom Jesus loved."

2.17   true

2.18   false

2.19   true

2.20   true

2.21   false

2.22   true

2.23   Any order:
   a. He stayed true to Jesus to the end.
   b. He cared for Jesus' mother, Mary.
   c. He encouraged Christians to love one another.

2.24   Either order:
   a. He remained and prayed with the disciples in the upper room.
   b. He stayed with the church during its persecution.

2.25   Adult check – possible answers:
   Setting: River Jordan
   What God Did or Said: Jesus invited John and Andrew to come and see where he was staying.
   What John Did or Said: From that point on, John followed Jesus as a disciple.
   John's Lesson to Us: We should not hesitate to follow Jesus wherever He may lead us.

2.26   Adult check – possible answers: enthusiastic, zealous, courageous, loving, tender

SECTION THREE

3.1 true

3.2 false

3.3 true

3.4 true

3.5 did all that the Lord commanded him

3.6 righteousness

3.7 600

3.8 Examples: God came first in Noah's life. He trusted God and was thankful to God for saving him, his family, and all the animals.

3.9 Adult check – possible answers:
Setting: The earth before the time of The Flood
What God Said or Did: God said Noah was the only righteous man in the whole generation. God told Noah to build an ark. God blessed Noah.
What Noah Said or Did: Noah did all that God commanded him to do.
Noah's Lesson to Us: We are to be righteous and obey God.

3.10 Adult check – examples: calm, courageous, faithful, humble, obedient, peaceful, reverent, trusting

3.11 Ruth was concerned about Naomi, her mother-in-law.

3.12 Example: Ruth thought of others before herself. She did not complain or feel sorry for herself.

3.13 She served God by loving and sacrificing for Naomi.

3.14 Adult check – possible answers:
Setting: Traveling from Moab to Bethlehem
What God Said or Did: The Lord dealt kindly with Ruth.

What Ruth Said or Did: Ruth said, "Whither thou goest I will go and where thou lodgest I will lodge."
Ruth's Lesson to Us: Ruth teaches us to be kind, helpful, and unselfish.

3.15 Examples: courageous, generous, kind, loyal, loving, thankful, trusting

3.16 Hannah was a woman of prayer when many had turned away from God.

3.17 The name Samuel means, "asked of God," and Hannah had prayed to God for a son.

3.18 a. My heart rejoiceth in the Lord.
b. There is none holy as the Lord.
c. There is none beside thee.

3.19 The Lord maketh poor and maketh rich.
or, He will keep the feet of his saints.

3.20 He shall give strength unto His King, and exalt the horn of his anointed.
or, The Lord shall judge the ends of the earth.

3.21 Adult check – possible answers:
Setting: In Ramah and Shiloh
What God Said or Did: God heard Hannah's prayer.
What Hannah Said or Did: Hannah prayed. She said that if God would give her a son, she would give the child to the Lord.
Hannah's Lesson to Us: When we praise God for His greatness, and when we thank Him, He adds even more blessings to our lives.

3.22 Adult check – examples: humble, loving, prayerful, reverent

3.23 He knew the storm would stop.

3.24 Rather then letting him drown, God sent a fish to swallow him. After three days, the fish vomited him up on dry land.

3.25 He obeyed.

3.26 Example – being merciful to Nineveh was more important than being concerned with the vine. If Jonah needed protection, the people of Nineveh did also.

3.27 repented

3.28 unhappy

3.29 gracious and merciful

3.30 Adult check – possible answers:
Setting: On a ship to Tarshish
What God Said or Did: God told Jonah to go preach to the city of Nineveh.
What Jonah Said or Did: Jonah ran from the Lord.
Jonah's Lesson to Us: God is not pleased when we disobey. God will teach us and correct us. God teaches us to tell other people about Him.

3.31 Jonah obeyed God and went to Nineveh a second time.

3.32 Example: Peter was strong, courageous, full of zeal and enthusiasm, sometimes fearful and doubting, bold, sometimes cowardly, rugged, tender-hearted, and sometimes impetuous.

3.33 Either order:
a. He stepped out of the boat to walk to Jesus on the water.
b. When many left Jesus, Peter declared that Jesus was the "Holy One of God."

3.34 Peter cut off a soldier's ear when Jesus was arrested. After the Resurrection, he was the first to go back to the fishing business.

3.35 Adult check – possible answers:
Setting: By the Sea of Galilee
What God Said or Did: God wanted Peter to be a fisher of men.
What Peter Said or Did: Peter became a great preacher and leader of souls for Jesus.

Peter's Lesson to Us: We are to be strong in the Lord and serve Jesus.

3.36 Examples: courageous, leader, persevering, zealous

3.37 Adult check

3.38 The men and women listed there believed God and acted on His promises.

3.39 Any order:
a. Walked with God
b. Claimed God's promises
c. Conquered enemies
d. Took a stand with God's people

3.40 The Christian should obey God.

3.41 race

3.42 Either order:
a. every weight
b. sin

3.43 look to Jesus

3.44 Adult check – examples: courageous, faithful, obedient, prayerful, trustful, persevering

SECTION ONE

1.1   invisible

1.2   spirit(s) *or* spirit beings

1.3   messenger

1.4   a. ministry
      b. ministering

1.5   real

1.6   Any order:
      a. Angels do not die.
      b. Angels do not get sick.
      c. Angels never sleep.

1.7   Either order:
      a. electricity
      b. wind

1.8   b

1.9   a

1.10 c

1.11 b

1.12 a

1.13 Examples: Angels can think, sing, obey, plan, and show emotions like people.

1.14 Any three:
      a. Gabriel flew from heaven and touched Daniel before he finished his prayer (Daniel 9:21).
      b. One angel killed 185,000 Assyrian soldiers to save the city of Jerusalem (2 Kings 19:35).
      c. An angel shut the lions' mouths for Daniel (Daniel 6:22).
      d. An angel rolled away the heavy stone from the door of Jesus' tomb (Matthew 28:2).

1.15 Any order:
      a. Angels are spirits.
      b. Angels are real.
      c. Angels are personal.
      d. Angels are supernatural.

1.16 true

1.17 true

1.18 false

1.19 true

1.20 false

1.21 true

1.22 false

1.23 host

1.24 a. thousand thousand
      b. ten thousand times ten thousand

1.25 a. multitude
      b. the host of heaven

1.26 God

1.27 evil

1.28 Jesus

1.29 temptation

1.30 Either order:
      a. prayer
      b. fasting

1.31 Adult check
      a. Word of God
      b. salvation
      c. faith
      d. righteousness
      e. truth
      f. Gospel of peace

SECTION TWO

2.1 nephew

2.2 men

2.3 Sodom

2.4 a. warned him
b. God was going to destroy it

2.5 sacrifice

2.6 angel

2.7 a. God
b. Jesus

2.8 twelve legions of angels

2.9 b

2.10 a

2.11 c

2.12 a

2.13 b

2.14 b

2.15 a

2.16 The name Peniel means "face of God." Jacob named the place Peniel where he met God in the form of angel and man because he had seen God face to face.

2.17 Israel means "he contends with God." The Lord changed Jacob's name to Israel after Jacob had wrestled with the angel.

2.18 Moses saw a bush that was on fire but did not burn up. The angel of the Lord appeared in the midst of the flame and spoke to Moses.

2.19 false

2.20 true

2.21 true

2.22 true

2.23 false

2.24 true

2.25 Example: Because Satan and evil spirits oppose God and His people, they want to harm, destroy, and even kill Christians, and therefore they plan dangers to harm people.

2.26 For he [God] shall give his angels charge over thee, to keep thee in all thy ways. They shall bear thee up in their hands, lest thou dash thy foot against a stone. (Psalm 91:11-12).
The angel of the Lord encampeth round about them that fear him, and delivereth them. (Psalm 34:7).

2.27 God sent an army of angels with horses and chariots of fire to encircle and protect Elisha.

2.28 God sent an angel of the Lord into the camp of the Assyrians and this angel killed 185,000 Assyrian soldiers.

2.29 c

2.30 d

2.31 g

2.32 f

2.33 i

2.34 h

2.35 a

2.36 Either order:
a. wise
b. handsome

2.37 a. chief minister
b. popular
c. successful

2.38 pray to King Darius for 30 days

2.39 praying to God three times a day

2.40 Example: King Darius believed that Daniel had a special relationship with God.

2.41 Example: The lions showed no interest in Daniel. They went about their routine as if Daniel were not there.

2.42 true

2.43 false

2.44 false

2.45 true

2.46 false

2.47 true

2.48 Example: The sailors were tired and discouraged and had lost all hope of reaching the shore alive.

2.49 Example: Paul probably felt strengthened, encouraged, and safe knowing that the angel of God was with him providing protection.

2.50 2

2.51 4

2.52 1

2.53 5

2.54 3

2.55 6

2.56 true

2.57 false

2.58 true

2.59 true

2.60 true

2.61 cares

2.62 ravens

2.63 widow

2.64 kill

2.65 angel

SECTION THREE

3.1 He refused to call on them for protection.

3.2 As the Son of God, He needed no direction.

3.3 Examples: Angels made announcements about Him. Angels strengthened Him after times of testing. Angels accompanied Him back to heaven after His earthly ministry.

3.4 false

3.5 true

3.6 true

3.7 Gabriel

3.8 Jesus

3.9 God

3.10 Example: Joseph was troubled by the strange events.

3.11 Example: Mary and Joseph both did as they were told to do.

3.12 4

3.13 3

3.14 5

3.15 2

3.16 1

3.17 They came to worship the King of the Jews.

3.18 Herod was afraid Christ would be his rival for the throne.

3.19 They were to stay until the angel told them to return.

3.20	b
3.21	a
3.22	c
3.23	b
3.24	c
3.25	false
3.26	true
3.27	false
3.28	false
3.29	kissing
3.30	sword
3.31	twelve legions
3.32	thine
3.33	Cross

3.34　Any order:
a. Angels rolled back the stone from Jesus' tomb.
b. Angels told the women that Christ was risen.
c. Angels told the women to tell the disciples.
d. Angels sat where Jesus had lain.

3.35　Jesus told the disciples to wait for the Holy Spirit to give them power to witness.

3.36　The angels said that Jesus would come in the same way He went into heaven.

3.37　Examples:
a. there was no room in the inn.
b. the king who had killed the babies was dead.
c. Peter did not have the faith to believe that Jesus could handle what was happening.

3.38　a. we know we can defeat Satan with the Scriptures
b. can be saved by believing on Him

SECTION ONE

1.1   false

1.2   true

1.3   false

1.4   false

1.5   here

1.6   you can only be in one place at a time

1.7   same

1.8   Yes
Any Bible quote:
Jeremiah 33:3 – Call unto me, and I will answer thee, and shew thee great and mighty things, which thou knowest not.
Psalm 145:18 – The LORD is nigh unto all them that call upon him, to all that call upon him in truth.
Acts 17:27–28 – That they should seek the Lord, if haply they might feel after him, and find him, though he be not far from every one of us: For in him we live, and move, and have our being; as certain also of your own poets have said, For we are also his offspring.

1.9   a. 1 Kings 8:30 – And hearken thou to the supplication of thy servant, and of thy people Israel, when they shall pray toward this place: and hear thou in heaven thy dwelling place: and when thou hearest, forgive.
b. Psalm 123:1 – Unto thee lift I up mine eyes, O thou that dwellest in the heavens.

1.10   Examples: God is spirit and a spirit cannot limited to just one place. A spirit can be present everywhere at once.

1.11   Wherever we go, God is there.

1.12   Any order:
a. beside
b. around
c. within

1.13   We can pray anywhere and anytime, and God will hear and help us.

1.14   Example: God is with me at this time.

1.15   Examples, any order:
a. speak
b. think
c. love
d. comfort

1.16   a. loved
b. love

1.17   true

1.18   the truth

1.19   Examples:
a. The sun comes up each morning.
b. Water boils at 212° F at sea level.
c. Arithmetic facts stay the same.

1.20   Example: What is true or false, good or bad one day will be the same the next day.

1.21   true

1.22   true

1.23   false

1.24   true

1.25   false

1.26   Any order:
a. God's love is everywhere.
b. God's truth is everywhere.
c. God's faithfulness is everywhere.
d. God's knowledge is everywhere.

1.27   O Lord, thou has searched me and known me. Thou knowest my downsitting and mine uprising, thou understandest my thought afar off.

1.28   Any order:
a. God is powerful.
b. God is holy.
c. God is good.

1.29   Adult check

1.30   God

SECTION TWO

2.1 people

2.2 a. Adam
b. Eve

2.3 a. judge
b. His love and mercy

2.4 The Tabernacle was a special place of meeting which reminded the people of God's presence. The people worshiped God in the Tabernacle.

2.5 a. 4
b. 2
c. 3
d. 1
e. 5

2.6 true

2.7 false

2.8 true

2.9 true

2.10 false

2.11 They would not worship an image of the king.

2.12 They believed God would be with them.

2.13 a. They were not burned.
b. Others believed in God.

2.14 storm

2.15 walking on the water

2.16 He brings peace.

2.17 Example: In the Old Testament, God was present in a special way in the Tabernacle. In the life of Christ, God revealed Himself in a special way in Christ. Today, every Christian has God dwelling within.

2.18 He wanted to win Indians to Christ.

2.19 He saved him from a rattlesnake.

2.20 Example: They saw how he trusted in God. They also saw how he loved God and loved them. They heard his message of God's love for them.

2.21 true

2.22 true

2.23 false

2.24 true

2.25 He was talking to God when he died.

2.26 Adult check

2.27 She was a very little person.

2.28 Example: She was very brave and believed God could do anything He promised.

2.29 Example: She witnessed to the Chinese people many times alone and trusted God to meet all her needs.

2.30 Example: People could see the power of God in her life as she bravely faced the prisoners, calmed them, and got them to discuss their problems.

2.31 something that gets in the way

2.32 people who are fleeing from their homes

2.33 Adult check

SECTION THREE

3.1 God heard his voice.

3.2 Example: It means to lean toward someone so as to be very near.

3.3 Examples – either order:
a. our needs, our feelings
b. our good deeds, our sins

3.4 Any order:
a. through the Bible
b. through conscience
c. through the Holy Spirit

3.5 Any order:
a. man
b. princes
c. chariots
d. horses

3.6 so God could live among men

3.7 because it was against God

3.8 The east is an unending or immeasurable distance from the west. Our sins are put an infinite distance from God.

3.9 Any order:
a. by making a person happy
b. by filling a person with goodness
c. by walking with a person

3.10 Examples; any order:
a. saves me
b. forgives me
c. satisfies me
d. is near me always
e. helps me
f. defends me
g. protects me
h. shelters me
i. encourages me
j. hears my prayers

3.11 false

3.12 true

3.13 true

3.14 false

3.15 Any order:
a. He never sleeps.
b. He is everywhere.
c. He knows hidden dangers.

3.16 Examples: God is able to lead and protect. He gives the sheep food and rest. He is good and merciful.

3.17 Psalm 116:1–2 – I love the Lord, because He hath heard my voice and my supplications. Because he hath inclined his ear unto me, therefore will I call upon Him as long as I live.

Adult check

3.18 a. God's nearness
b. He leans close to a person.
c. He listens carefully.

SECTION ONE

1.1   book

1.2   most loving Father

1.3   a. forty-one
      b. more than a thousand

1.4   inspired

1.5   author

1.6   Any order:
      a. kings
      b. shepherds
      c. poets
      d. fishermen
      e. doctors
      f. military leaders
      g. scholars
      Also, statesmen, philosophers

1.7   Any order:
      a. It is he most important book in the world (the Book of books)
      b. It is the largest-selling book in the world.
      c. It was the first book to be printed (in 1455 by Johannes Gutenburg).
      d. It has been translated into more languages than any other book.

1.8   Any order:
      a. It has basic unity of various parts in telling the truth about God and man.
      b. It has one main author: God.
      c. It has one great theme: God's loving plan of salvation.
      Also, It has one main character: Jesus Christ. It has one basic purpose: reveal the Word of God and the plan of salvation to man.

1.9   Adult check

1.10   Adult check

1.11   a. hope
       b. fulfillment

1.12   Either order:
       a. heaven
       b. earth

1.13   a. the garden of Eden
       b. bay by Bethlehem
       c. Revelation

1.14   Adult check

1.15   Adult check

1.16   Protestant: 66 books
       Roman Catholic or Orthodox: 73 or more

1.17   Genesis

1.18   Revelation

1.19   150

1.20   176

1.21   2

1.22   Old Testament

1.23   Examples: car, door, wheels
                house, roof, walls
                school, teacher, students

1.24   a. builder
       b. cook
       c. an author

1.25   f

1.26   d

1.27   a

1.28   e

1.29   c

1.30   a covenant or agreement

1.31   God's loving plan of salvation, or the story of redemption

1.32   Example: Jesus was foretold in the Old Testament books and prophets. The New Testament tells the story of Jesus Christ and how the Gospel was carried to the ends of the earth.

1.33 Depends upon the translation of the Bible used. Example from (JKJV):
a. law of the LORD
b. testimonies
c. his ways
d. precepts
e. statutes
f. commandments
g. righteous judgments

1.34 irregular

1.35 overflow

1.36 non-Christian

1.37 coexist

1.38 illegible

SECTION TWO

2.1 a. History
b. Poetry
c. Prophecy

2.2 a. Torah (Law of Moses)
b. Prophets
c. Writings

2.3 Jesus

2.4 a. Genesis
b. Exodus
c. Leviticus
d. Numbers
e. Joshua
f. Judges
g. Ruth
h. 1 Samuel
i. 1 Kings
j. 2 Chronicles
k. Ezra
l. Esther

2.5 Adult check

2.6 The Lord is my shepherd; I shall not want.

2.7 Adult check

2.8 Adult check

2.9 Genesis

2.10 Abraham

2.11 famine

2.12 Ten Commandments

2.13 choose

2.14 a. 5
b. 2
c. 6
d. 4
e. 3
f. 1

2.15 Example: Joshua was chosen by God to lead the people of Israel into Caanan, the Promised land. Under Joshua, Israel overcame many enemies and settled the Promised land. Near the end of his life, he told the people to choose the God they would serve.

2.16 a. 3
b. 1
c. 4
d. 2

2.17 Samuel

2.18 kings

2.19 a. Saul
b. pride

2.20 Example: "A man after His own heart" probably means a man who loves God and puts God first in his life. It probably means a man who trusts God enough to do whatever God commands.

2.21 d

2.22   c

2.23   g

2.24   a

2.25   e

2.26   Either order:
a. the building of the Temple
b. the kingdom was divided

2.27   Their sin of turning away from God

2.28   Adult check

2.29   Adult check

2.30   Adult check

2.31   Adult check

2.32   false

2.33   true

2.34   true

2.35   false

2.36   false

2.37   Example: The book of Ecclesiastes teaches that life without God at the center is empty and worthless. It tells young people to remember their Creator while they are young.

2.38   a. Isaiah
b. Jeremiah
c. Ezekiel
d. Daniel
e. Hosea
f. Joel
g. Amos
h. Jonah
i. Micah
j. Haggai
k. Zechariah
l. Malachi

2.39   Adult check

2.40   a. The Old Testament supports the New Testament.

b. The New Testament completes the Old Testament.

c. The Old Testament is incomplete without the New Testament.

2.41   The Old Testament had to come first because a roof (the New Testament) had to have support.

2.42   Example: The Old Testament tells us that Jesus Christ would come to earth for our salvation.

2.43   Adult check

SECTION THREE

3.1 Adult check

3.2 a. Gospels
b. History
c. Epistles
d. Prophecy

3.3 a. Matthew
b. Mark
c. Luke
d. John
e. Acts
f. Romans
g. Galatians
h. Ephesians
i. Titus
j. Hebrews
k. James
l. Revelation

3.4 Adult check

3.5 Ιησους Χριστος εχθες και σημερον ο αυτος και εις τους αιωνας.

3.6 Ιησους Χριστος

3.7 Any order:
a. papyrus
b. wood
c. stone
d. leather

3.8 Either order:
a. iron tools
b. knives
or pens made from reeds

3.9 4

3.10 3

3.11 c

3.12 d

3.13 b

3.14 a

3.15 Luke 2:40 – And the child grew, and waxed strong in spirit, filled with wisdom: and the grace of God was upon him.

Luke 2:52 – And Jesus increased in wisdom and stature, and in favour with God and man.

3.16 Adult check

3.17 1

3.18 5

3.19 2

3.20 6

3.21 4

3.22 Dead

3.23 Judea

3.24 Galilee

3.25 Galilee

3.26 Adult check

3.27 a wedding in Cana

3.28 he must be born again

3.29 healed a blind man

3.30 Sermon on the Mount

3.31 healed a leper; called Matthew; healed a withered hand; many followed Jesus; chose twelve apostles; parables of sower, tares, pearl; called Simon, Andrew, James, and John

3.32 fed the 5,000

3.33 false

3.34 true

3.35 true

3.36 true

3.37 false

3.38 true

3.39 But ye shall receive power, after that the Holy Ghost is come upon you: and ye shall be witnesses unto me both in Jerusalem, and in all Judaea, and in Samaria, and unto the uttermost part of the earth.

3.40 In Jerusalem:

Acts 2:1-6	Holy Spirit came
Acts 2:14-38	Peter's sermon
Acts 2:41	3,000 people added
Acts 2:42-47	Loved each other
Acts 3:1-9	Lame man healed
Acts 4:4	5,000 people added
Acts 7:54-60	Stephen killed
Acts 8:4	Christians scatter

In Judea and Samaria:

Acts 9:1-6	Saul converted
Acts 9:18	Saul baptized
Acts 10:9-15	Peter's vision
Acts 12:4	Peter in prison
Acts 12:5	Praying for Peter
Acts 12:23	Death of Herod

In the Uttermost Part of the Earth:

Acts 13:2-3	First missionary journey begins
Acts 15:36	Second missionary journey begins
Acts 18:23	Third missionary journey begins
Acts 24:1	Paul before Felix
Acts 26:1	Paul before Agrippa
Acts 27:14-44	Paul's shipwreck
Acts 28:16	Arrives at Rome

3.41 Adult check

3.42 Adult check

3.43 twenty-one

3.44 thirteen

3.45 Either order:
a. to tell them he would visit them
b. to explain the Gospel

3.46 a. sinned
b. short
c. God
d. justified
e. faith
f. peace
g. Lord Jesus Christ
h. present
i. bodies

3.47 Adult check

3.48 Adult check

3.49 Adult check

3.50 Adult check

3.51 better

3.52 doers

3.53 suffering

3.54 a. believe
b. love

3.55 falling

3.56 true

3.57 true

3.58 false

3.59 false

3.60 true

3.61 false

3.62 true

SECTION ONE

1.1 relationships

1.2 holy life

1.3 Any order:
a. home
b. church
c. school
d. work

1.4 family *or* home

1.5 Wisdom

1.6 a. parents
b. children

1.7 Either order:
a. love God
b. love one another

1.8 The fear of the LORD is the beginning of wisdom: and the knowledge of the holy is understanding.

1.9 For the family members to love one another.

1.10 Either order:
a. mercy
b. truth

1.11 Any order:
a. suffereth long
b. is kind
c. envieth not
d. vaunteth not itself - or - is not puffed up
e. doth not behave itself unseemly
f. seeketh not her own
g. not easily provoked
h. thinketh no evil
i. rejoiceth not in iniquity
j. rejoiceth in the truth
k. beareth all things
l. believeth all things
m. hopeth all things
n. endureth all things

1.12 Example: Listening is an important method of learning. It is also a way to show respect. Children can hear and learn about Jesus Christ if they listen to their parents.

1.13 Example: You can hear and understand without obeying. If you hear and understand and then do what you were told, that is obedience.

1.14 false

1.15 true

1.16 false

1.17 true

1.18 Any order:
a. food
b. clothing
c. shelter

1.19 loves

1.20 loved

1.21 Either order:
a. words
b. physical; spanking

1.22 Example: Parents are to teach and build good habits in their children. This training will develop character in the child. This character determines the way of life.

1.23 b. have a duty

1.24 c. love

1.25 Train up a child in the way he should go: and when he is old, he will not depart from it.

1.26 Even a child is known by his doings, whether his work be pure, and whether it be right.

1.27	b	1.37	a
1.28	c	1.38	a and b

1.29 b

1.30 c

1.31 a and b

1.32 c

1.33 b

1.34 b

1.35 c

1.36 c

1.39 I. Relationships in the Home
       A. Introduction
       B. Loving Others
       C. Hearing and Obeying
           Instruction
           1. A place to listen and learn
           2. A place to obey
       D. Receiving Correction
       E. Learning Correct Behavior

SECTION TWO

2.1 Example: It would be very displeasing if one or more of the members caused dissension among other members of the church.

2.2 A new commandment I give unto you, That ye love one another; as I have loved you, that ye also love one another.

2.3 Adult check

2.4 grow

2.5 walketh

2.6 neglect

2.7 a. pastors
     b. teachers

2.8 hold

2.9 II. Relationships in the Church
     A. Introduction
     B. Loving our Brothers and Sisters
        in Christ
     C. Growing in Christ
     D. Giving and Receiving Support

2.10 Any order:
(1) love one another
(2) not cause dissension
(3) grow in Christ
(4) be faithful to regular attendance when the church meets
(5) receive instruction from ministers and teachers in the church
(6) financially support the ministers and ministries of the church
(7) help others in the church who are in need or want
Also, use and exercise spiritual gifts

SECTION THREE

3.1 love

3.2 Any order:
a. hatred
b. envy
c. jealousy or bitterness

3.3 They can strengthen us and encourage us.

3.4 c

3.5 a

3.6 d

3.7 b

3.8 Example: With love, honesty, and kindness, the Christian may be a witness to the non-Christian.

3.9 Any order:
a. give advice
b. give help
c. be there when needed

3.10 e

3.11 g

3.12 a

3.13 f

3.14 b

3.15 genuine

3.16 hates

3.17 Examples, any order:
a. with words
b. not keeping promises
c. copying answers

3.18 Examples: lie to parents, friends, others

3.19 No. A half-lie can hurt as much as a complete lie.

3.20 Either order:
a. become a better person
b. be a testimony

3.21 b

3.22 a

3.23 Examples: Pray and ask Jesus to help you be consistent in what you do and say. Be truthful and consistent in your relationships with others.

3.24 Happiness and cheerfulness must come from the heart or inside of a person.

3.25 Adult check

3.26 Example: Sin centers around self, but Christ humbles us when we receive Him.

3.27 Examples:
a. "You played a great game!"
b. "You sure played well!"

3.28 Examples:
a. "That was a good game."
b. "You were a good opponent."

3.29 b

3.30 a

3.31 c

3.32 a

3.33 Example: Think about what you say.

3.34 Example: It dishonors the Lord.

3.35-36 Adult check

3.37 true

3.38 false

3.39 false

3.40 true

3.41 My son, if sinners entice thee, consent thou not.

3.42 Any of the following verses could be written: 1 Peter 4:15; 1 Thessalonians 4:15; Proverbs 26:17

3.43 hate

3.44 lose

3.45 bad

3.46 enemy

3.47 false

3.48 humble

SECTION FOUR

4.1 wisdom

4.2 understanding

4.3 a. all your heart
b. own understanding
c. your ways
d. make your paths straight

4.4 a. Jesus
b. others
c. yourself

4.5 happiness

4.6 God will repay with interest

4.7 Proverbs 9:10

4.8 Proverbs 3:6

4.9 Proverbs 14:31

4.10 Proverbs 19:17

4.11 true

4.12 false

4.13 true

4.14 true

4.15 false

4.16 true

4.17 true

4.18 true

4.19 sword

4.20 soft

4.21 pleasant

4.22 Example: A business person uses false measurements to make more profits.

4.23 Example: The person who makes great profit by cheating loses peace of mind; *or* They are troubled by their conscience.

4.24 Examples:
a. giving jobs to people they like
b. treating some people more kindly than others
c. giving better deals to people they like

4.25 Examples:
Jesus' choices for us:
a. new life in Christ
b. friendship with God
c. service for God

A greedy person's choices:
a. making money
b. collecting things
c. controlling his own life

4.26 Example: God does not say that having riches is wrong. God says we are not to trust in riches. He also says that we are not to put material things first in our lives.

4.27 Example: Some people in authority use cruelty to show their power and control.

4.28 Example: Becoming angry easily makes people do and say foolish things.

4.29 yield

4.30 a. city
b. wall

4.31 Example: A person's reputation is how he is known by other people. His reputation is how other people think he is. He usually gets his reputation from the way he acts and talks.

4.32 b

4.33 c

4.34 Adult check

4.35 Trust in the LORD with all thine heart; and lean not unto thine own understanding. In all thy ways acknowledge him, and he shall direct thy paths.

4.36 Adult check

4.37 think about

4.38 standard

4.39 not lazy

SECTION ONE

1.1 Any order:
a. the Bible as God's Word
b. God's Creation of the world
c. the Resurrection of Jesus Christ

1.2 Example: Christians should always be ready to defend their faith, but they should do it with gentleness and reverence.

1.3 Example: Christians believe the Bible is God's Word and that the books of the Old and New Testaments contain the Word of God. Christians also believe that the Bible is inspired by God and that God is the true author.

1.4 It is important because the Bible is the basis for many of our other beliefs about God and Jesus Christ.

1.5 In the Bible itself

1.6 Example: It says that all Scripture (the Bible) is inspired by God. This means that God is the real author of the Bible; therefore, the Bible is God's Word.

1.7 Adult check

1.8 true

1.9 false

1.10 true

1.11 true

1.12 true

1.13 Example: One source of evidence is that the Bible claims to be inspired by God with God as its true author (2 Timothy 3:16-17). The second source of evidence in the Bible that it is God's Word is the ample evidence throughout the Bible of the voice of God being recorded. In addition, many references in The Bible refer to God speaking to people of the Bible.

1.14 All scripture is given by inspiration of God, and is profitable for doctrine, for reproof, for correction, for instruction in righteousness: That the man of God may be perfect, throughly furnished unto all good works.

1.15 f

1.16 e

1.17 d

1.18 a

1.19 c

1.20 Example: The characteristics of the Bible have to with things we can observe about the Bible. The Bible is different from all other books ever written. It has so many different human authors over such a long period of time, yet it tells one continuous story. Also, the Bible has unity and continuity. It was written in different languages, in different forms of writing, in many different places, yet it tells one continuous story. Finally, the Bible has harmony from beginning to end. Each part of the Bible agrees with every other part. All of these characteristics give evidence that God is the true author behind the writing of the Bible.

1.21 a. But thou, Bethlehem Ephratah, though thou be little among the thousands of Judah, yet out of thee shall he come forth unto me that is to be ruler in Israel; whose goings forth have been from of old, from everlasting.
b. For unto us a child is born, unto us a son is given: and the government shall be upon his shoulder: and his name shall be called Wonderful, Counsellor, The mighty God, The everlasting Father, The Prince of Peace.

c. Then the eyes of the blind shall be opened, and the ears of the deaf shall be unstopped.

d. I am poured out like water, and all my bones are out of joint: my heart is like wax; it is melted in the midst of my bowels.

e. For thou wilt not leave my soul in hell; neither wilt thou suffer thine Holy One to see corruption.

1.22 false

1.23 true

1.24 true

1.25 false

1.26 true

1.27 false

1.28 Any order:
a. Superiority.
Example: Its superiority is demonstrated when compared with other books, even other books of religion. It has superior ability to give and predict the truth. It is inerrant.
b. Popularity.
Example: It has been circulated, reprinted, translated, and read more than any other book in the world. No other book has such popularity.
c. Stability.
Example: The Bible has suffered more attacks, criticism, and opposition than any other book in history, yet it has survived all attempts to destroy it.

1.29 Example: Many people are enemies of God. Many people do not wish to believe the Bible.

1.30 Example: By surviving attempts to destroy it, the Bible disproved its enemies.

1.31 the influence of the Bible to the world

1.32 The Bible is God's influence that flows to the world.

1.33 Examples; any order:
a. art
b. music
c. law
d. literature or language development, education

1.34 c

1.35 e

1.36 h

1.37 b

1.38 a

1.39 g

1.40 God

1.41 seed

1.42 Examples – any order:
a. to produce good results—good fruit
b. to guide him
c. to cleanse him
d. to make him wise
Also, to help him rejoice, to enlighten him

1.43 (1) Examples:
a. commandment of the LORD
b. pure
c. enlightens the eyes

(2) Examples:
a. statutes of the LORD
b. right
c. rejoices the heart

1.44 The law of the LORD is perfect, converting the soul: the testimony of the LORD is sure, making wise the simple. The statutes of the LORD are right, rejoicing the heart: the commandment of the LORD is pure, enlightening the eyes. The fear of the LORD is clean, enduring for ever: the judgments of the LORD are true and righteous altogether.

1.45   For the word of God is quick, and powerful, and sharper than any twoedged sword, piercing even to the dividing asunder of soul and spirit, and of the joints and marrow, and is a discerner of the thoughts and intents of the heart.

SECTION TWO

2.1   true

2.2   true

2.3   false

2.4   true

2.5   false

2.6   true

2.7   false

2.8   Either order:
   a. the number of the stars cannot be counted
   b. the stars and the sun are their own sources of light and are the same material

2.9   d

2.10 c

2.11 g

2.12 e

2.13 f

2.14 Any order:
   a. vegetation in undigested food of a frozen, extinct mammal in Siberia was not like any surrounding vegetation for ten thousand miles
   b. Fossils of tropical plants and animals discovered by Admiral Byrd at South Pole
   c. Tropical fruit tree, uprooted and found by researchers in New Siberian Islands

2.15 true

2.16 true

2.17 true

2.18 true

2.19 true

2.20 theistic evolution

2.21 intelligent design

2.22 before

2.23 chance

2.24 Any order:
   a. They believe that the earth's atmosphere never changed.
   b. They believe in an unknown first life organism
   c. They believe in the theory that life began in the ocean.
   d. They believe that life evolved from simple life-form to the more complex.

2.25 a. dead animals carry disease
   b. do not eat blood
   c. unclean meat or food is to be burned
   d. infected sores transmit disease
   e. spit is unsanitary
   f. do not eat dead animals

2.26 c

2.27 b

2.28 d

2.29 a

2.30 b

SECTION THREE

3.1 true

3.2 true

3.3 true

3.4 false

3.5 predicted

3.6 David

3.7 Acts

3.8 a. And while they abode in Galilee, Jesus said unto them, The Son of man shall be betrayed into the hands of men: And they shall kill him, and the third day he shall be raised again. And they were exceeding sorry.
b. And he began to teach them, that the Son of man must suffer many things, and be rejected of the elders, and of the chief priests, and scribes, and be killed, and after three days rise again.
c. A little while, and ye shall not see me: and again, a little while, and ye shall see me, because I go to the Father.

3.9 Either order:
a. He knew the Old Testament prophecies.
b. He was the Son of God.

3.10 The angel appeared to the women and told them.

3.11 4

3.12 1

3.13 5

3.14 2

3.15 3

3.16 Either order:
a. the stone
b. the guards

3.17 Example: The guards were given money by the chief priests and elders to lie about the missing body of Jesus. They lied, saying that Jesus' disciples had stolen His body.

3.18 b

3.19 c

3.20 d

3.21 d

3.22 Example: The fact that the sealed and closely guarded tomb was empty is an unusual event. It alone should prove that Jesus was resurrected.

3.23 false

3.24 true

3.25 false

3.26 true

3.27 false

3.28 true

3.29 Example: They thought He had been killed and would not be with them again. They were glad to see that He was alive and was with them again.

3.30 Example: to show the disciples that He was Jesus by performing a miracle

3.31 500

3.32 believer

3.33 ascend

3.34 b

3.35 e

3.36 a

3.37 c

3.38 a. enemy of Christ
b. believer

3.39 a. angry
b. peaceful

3.40 a. fearful
      b. bold

3.41 a. bragging

      b. humble

3.42 Faith in the resurrected Christ changed their lives.

3.43 He saw Jesus alive.

3.44 The Greeks had difficulty receiving the message; however, a few believed the message and became followers of Paul.

3.45 a. 4

      b. 2

      c. 6

      d. 1

      e. 5

      f. 3

3.46 a. believed

      b. the disciples were discouraged

      c. they were sad

      d. they were victorious

      e. they were glad

3.47 Adult check

SECTION ONE

1.1　a. Rome
　　　b. Tarsus

1.2　rights

1.3　a. Jew
　　　b. Jewish

1.4　synagogues

1.5　a. Rome
　　　b. Jew
　　　c. synagogues

1.6　But sanctify the Lord God in your hearts: and be ready always to give an answer to every man that asketh you a reason of the hope that is in you with meekness and fear:

1.7　education

1.8　a. Gamaliel
　　　b. Jerusalem

1.9　Pharisee

1.10　Either order:
　　　a. Greek
　　　b. Hebrew

1.11　Old Testament

1.12　a. witness
　　　b. Greeks

1.13　Example: We must study hard to be able to witness to others. (1 Peter 3:15)

1.14　d

1.15　f

1.16　g

1.17　c

1.18　a

1.19　b

1.20　e

1.21　five

1.22　thirteen

1.23　Either order:
　　　a. big
　　　b. strong

1.24　Any order:
　　　a. smart
　　　b. warm
　　　c. friendly
　　　d. enthusiastic

1.25　big cities

1.26　b

1.27　a

1.28　b

1.29　b

1.30　c

1.31　a

1.32　c

1.33　Paul planned to imprison the Christians there.

1.34　Christ appeared to Paul on the Damascus Road.

1.35　The light blinded Paul.

1.36　Paul stayed with Judas on the street called "Straight."

1.37　God healed Paul through Ananias.

1.38　the Law *or* the Mosaic Law

1.39　Jesus Christ

1.40　a. schoolmaster
　　　b. Christ

1.41　a. alive
　　　b. provision

1.42　Jesus

1.43　Gentiles

1.44　9

1.45	6		1.61	abstract
1.46	5		1.62	concrete
1.47	2		1.63	abstract
1.48	1		1.64	concrete
1.49	3		1.65	concrete
1.50	8		1.66	concrete
1.51	4		1.67	abstract
1.52	7		1.68	abstract
1.53	Adult check		1.69	abstract
1.54	Rome renamed it Palestine		1.70	concrete
1.55	It was named after the Philistines		1.71	concrete
1.56	concrete		1.72	abstract
1.57	abstract		1.73	abstract
1.58	concrete		1.74	concrete
1.59	abstract		1.75	abstract
1.60	abstract		1.76	Adult check

SECTION TWO

2.1   Holy Spirit

2.2   John Mark

2.3   on the east of Cyprus

2.4   island of Cyprus

2.5   Paphos

2.6   synagogues

2.7   Paul

2.8   A change in leadership had taken place. The two missionaries were now thinking about going directly to the Gentiles.

2.9   e

2.10 d

2.11 a

2.12 f

2.13 c

2.14 a. Antioch
      b. Pisidia

2.15 Asia Minor

2.16 The Gentiles showed great interest.

2.17 Almost the whole town turned out.

2.18 They said that their message was blasphemy and caused the government to persecute them.

2.19 Paul preached to the Jews, then the Gentiles. The Jews would persecute him and he would flee.

2.20 It was worth it because the result of his preaching was that the gentiles would gain salvation.

2.21 The word of God was spread and many believed.

2.22 a. light of the Gentiles
      b. salvation

2.23 true

2.24 false

2.25 true

2.26 false

2.27 true

2.28 true

2.29 false

2.30 true

2.31 a. The apostles went to Lystra, then to Derbe, then back to Lystra.
      b. The Roman government allowed the Jewish people to worship in their own way.
      c. In Lystra, Paul healed a crippled man.

2.32 They were to receive eternal life through Christ.

2.33 It was different in approach, not in doctrine.

2.34 Paul always preached first in the synagogues.

2.35 Example: They were to be fellow heirs, part of the same body, and partakers of the promise.

2.36 The actions of Paul and Barnabas and their approach of ministering directly to the Gentiles were debated in the Jerusalem church.

2.37 They needed explanation of what the Jews were claiming against them.

2.38 1) Was it right to preach the gospel to the Gentiles?
      2) Was it necessary for Gentile Christians to obey the Jewish law?

2.39 They thought that the believers should obey the Mosaic laws to the letter.

2.40 They were less strict and didn't have many rules for Gentile believers.

2.41 a. everything associated with idolatry
b. all types of immorality
c. eating meat from animals killed by strangulation
d. eating blood

2.42 through the grace of God, by faith in Jesus Christ

2.43 a. the Gentile and Jewish missions could exist side by side
b. Paul's mission was made clearer
c. The Jews began to be persecuted

2.44 They disagreed about taking Mark or leaving him.

2.45 God made two teams instead of one.

2.46 They went to Cyprus.

2.47 a. Asia Minor
b. Silas

2.48 Silvanus

2.49 unity

2.50 a. Roman citizen
b. Gentiles
c. the attitudes of the church at Jerusalem

2.51 strengthened

2.52 Timothy

2.53 a. half
b. Greek

2.54 Jewish Christian

2.55 Adult check

2.56 a. Troas
b. Aegean Sea

2.57 He saw a man from Macedonia say, "Come over to Macedonia and help us."

2.58 Luke

2.59 Luke

2.60 true

2.61 false

2.62 false

2.63 true

2.64 true

2.65 Paul had cast out the demon and ruined their business.

2.66 An earthquake opened the jail cells.

2.67 The jailkeeper and his family were saved that night.

2.68 a. idolatry
b. world
c. man
d. Jesus Christ

2.69 a. Dionysius (any order)
b. Damaris
c. a few others

2.70 a. Athens (either order)
b. Corinth

2.71 Gallio

2.72 Nothing. He gave Paul full freedom.

2.73 one and one-half years

2.74 Aquila and Priscilla

2.75 Any of the following: He wrote the two letters while he was at Corinth. He made tents. He preached in the synagogues.

2.76 He wanted to explain the return of Christ to those who were confused about His return.

2.77 Example: Believers were still confused about Christ's return.

2.78 Paul's headquarters were with Titus Justus.

2.79 Crispus was the head of the synagogue.

2.80 Aquila and Priscilla went with the missionaries.

2.81   Paul stayed only a short time at Ephesus.

2.82   They stopped at Caesarea and Jerusalem.

2.83   a

2.84   b

2.85   a

2.86-88 Examples:

2.86   interesting

2.87   furious; was angered to action

2.88   a witness; a living Bible

SECTION THREE

3.1   the church at Ephesus

3.2   Either order:
a. Galatia
b. Phrygia

3.3   Either order
a. from tourists that come to see the temple
b. from trade done at the seaport

3.4   Diana

3.5   fewer tourists were coming and people were no longer buying the little idols

3.6   Demetrius

3.7   The mob did not know the difference between the Jewish religion and Christianity because both taught there is only one God.

3.8   the town clerk

3.9   The townspeople should take the matter (or the Christians) to court.

3.10   3 years

3.11   3 months

3.12   all of Asia, both Jews and Greeks

3.13   Miracles were performed; demons were cast out; and many magicians burned their books and quit their works.

3.14   beasts

3.15   They risked their lives for Paul.

3.16   Macedonia

3.17   a. Ephesus
b. Macedonia

3.18   go to Corinth personally

3.19   for three months

3.20   the offering Paul collected in Asia and Macedonia

3.21   Example: He introduced himself in the letter and explained the gospel in great detail and order. He prepared the way for his coming and shared with them his plans for that part of the world.

3.22   There was a plot to kill Paul when he went to the ship.

3.23   Paul kept the Passover in Philippi.

3.24   He fell asleep and fell three stories to the ground.

3.25   Paul wanted to be in Jerusalem for the day of Pentecost.

3.26   true

3.27   false

3.28   true

3.29   true

3.30   true

3.31   false

3.32   false

3.33   I have fought a good fight, I have finished my course, I have kept the faith.

3.34   Jesus Christ and him crucified

3.35   in Christ

3.36   no one *or* only Jesus

3.37   to show us our need of Jesus

3.38   Example: Christ is the Lord—the God-man—not just a teacher or prophet. He is God and Savior.

3.39   Example: He fulfilled the Law for us. He paid the penalty of the law and became our righteousness.

3.40   a. the law of Christ
       b. the mind of Christ
       c. love of Christ

3.41   a. new creatures
       b. His spirit

3.42   We are in Christ and with other believers as members of the same family.

3.43   The climax of God's plan is the Second Coming of Christ.

3.44   the spiritual part

3.45   by letting Christ live in us

3.46   Holy Spirit

3.47   a. family
       b. equal
       c. purpose

3.48   Any order:
       a. home
       b. church
       c. school

3.49   Any order:
       a. We can witness everywhere.
       b. We can study the Bible.
       c. We can do everything in love.

3.50   b

3.51   a

3.52   a

3.53   b

3.54   a

3.55   Cornelius'

3.56   Lydia's

3.57   Paul's

3.58   rulers'

3.59   Peoples'

3.60   Adult check

SECTION ONE

1.1	false
1.2	true
1.3	false
1.4	false
1.5	true
1.6	Adult check
1.7	c
1.8	e
1.9	d
1.10	a
1.11	Adult check
1.12	Adult check
1.13	Adult check

1.14 **Across:**
    6. obedient
    7. John
    9. spirit
    12. race
    14. battle
    15. sin
    19. Nicodemus
    21. your
    22. snail

Down:
    1. scholar
    2. died
    3. patience
    4. Son
    5. Jew
    8. grow
    10. Paul
    11. train
    13. eternity
    14. Bible
    16. God
    17. Jesus
    18. run
    20. all

1.15	noun
1.16	adjective
1.17	verb
1.18	adjective
1.19	verb
1.20	adjective
1.21	noun
1.22	verb
1.23	adjective
1.24	noun
1.25	c
1.26	d
1.27	a
1.28	b
1.29	c
1.30	true
1.31	true
1.32	true
1.33	false
1.34	true
1.35	Adult check

Example: The disciples and Jesus were crossing the Sea of Galilee in a boat. Jesus was sleeping when a great storm came upon the sea. The disciples were afraid and woke up Jesus. Jesus stood up and said, "Peace, be still." The sea became calm. The disciples were amazed that even the winds and the sea obeyed Jesus.

1.36   Adult check

SECTION TWO

2.1 Examples: (any order)
a. God is perfect and just.
b. Man has a conscience to know right from wrong.
c. Man has the ability to choose right from wrong.
or Man is responsible for his choices.
God has given man a soul.

2.2 God is perfect and He has appointed Christ as our judge. Christ knows everything about us.

2.3 false

2.4 false

2.5 true

2.6 true

2.7 false

2.8 false

2.9 false

2.10 false

2.11 false

2.12 false

2.13 false

2.14 true

2.15 The *bema* was the seat of the judge in the athletic contests of Ancient Greece. The *bema* was high above the other seats so that the judge could see well.

2.16 Those works which were done because of love for God, works which bring honor and glory to God will be rewarded.

2.17 b

2.18 b

2.19 c

2.20 b

2.21 a

2.22 Every man's work will be revealed by fire. Fire will try every man's work.

2.23 crowns

2.24 God

2.25 life

2.26 glory

2.27 Any order:
a. feed the flock—spiritual food
b. be a leader
c. set a good example

2.28 d

2.29 b

2.30 a

2.31 c

2.32 Any order:
a. Rewards will be given only to Christians who have honored and glorified God.
b. Jesus will be the judge and giver of rewards.
c. Your rewards will bring glory to God through eternity.
d. Your rewards will last through eternity.

2.33 life

2.34 righteousness

2.35 glory

2.36 rejoicing

SECTION THREE

3.1 Adult check
Example: John saw a great white throne with many people trying to run away, but there was no place for them to hide. The graves and the sea delivered up their dead, important and unimportant, rich and poor, and they were judged by their works. Those whose names were not written in the Book of Life were thrown into the lake of fire.

3.2 on the island of Patmos

3.3 to reveal what events will take place at the end of time on earth

3.4 destructive, able to destroy

3.5 scholarship, a grant of money to help a student continue his education

3.6 Example:
The unsaved will spend eternity without the love, joy, and peace of God. There will be much sorry, crying, and pain in hell.

3.7 Adult check

SECTION ONE

1.1 God has ultimate authority over all creation because He created everything that exists, and He is all-powerful.

1.2 Any order:
a. creation
b. the Scriptures
c. His Son, Jesus Christ

1.3 Either order:
a. A potter has the rights and freedom of a creator to form the clay in whatever way he wants.
b. Once the pottery is formed, the potter also has the right and freedom to do with it as he pleases.

1.4 eternal

1.5 Either order:
a. laws of nature
b. divine law

1.6 nature

1.7 instinct

1.8 divine

1.9 Natural

1.10 Holy Bible

1.11 Examples – either order:
a. Planets revolve around the sun in set paths and times that remain the same.
b. The earth's rotation around its axis gives us day and night.

1.12 Example: God divided the Red Sea so that the Israelites could escape from the Egyptians (Exodus, Chapter 14).

1.13 true

1.14 false

1.15 false

1.16 true

1.17 false

1.18 Example: Jesus was obedient to God the Father because He had complete respect for God's authority.

1.19 c

1.20 a

1.21 a

1.22 Scriptures

1.23 a. truth
b. word

1.24 Example: Jesus upheld the authority of the Scriptures. He often began His teaching using Old Testament Scriptures. Jesus also put His seal of approval on the future New Testament writings and gave them His authority before they were written.

1.25 He is our Comforter.
He guides us.
He strengthens us.
He gives us power.

1.26 b

1.27 c

1.28 a

1.29 e

1.30 f

1.31 false

1.32 true

1.33 true

1.34 false

1.35 true

1.36 false

1.37 true

1.38   Example: The Holy Spirit gives us the power to follow Jesus and to live a life pleasing to God.

1.39   Example: The Holy Spirit strengthens us inwardly. He helps us to live the law of love and to live God's will, even when it is difficult.

SECTION TWO

2.1   a. own
       b. image
       c. them
       d. them
       e. them

2.2   because God has delegated part of His authority to the family

2.3   GOD

       FATHER/MOTHER

            CHILDREN

2.4   Either order:
       a. age
       b. ability

2.5   wisely

2.6   authority

2.7   parents

2.8   parents

2.9   true

2.10   true

2.11   a. relatives
       b. sitters
       c. community and government
       d. schools
       e. organizations
       f. churches

2.12   Adult check

2.13   a. Train you and teach you God's ways
       c. Provide food, clothing, and shelter
       e. Provide a calm and loving home

2.14   c. Honor and obey your parents
       d. Accept your parents' decisions
       e. Help your parents in every way possible

2.15   the right to have some time alone

2.16   Examples:
       a. Do my chores without being told
       b. Keep my room clean
       c. Obey my parents
       or, Listen to my parents' advice.
       Say "thank you" and tell them I love them.

2.17   false

2.18   true

2.19   true

2.20   true

2.21   false

2.22   b, a

2.23   b, a

2.24   b, a

2.25   b, a

2.26   b, a

SECTION THREE

3.1   Any order:
      a. order
      b. safety
      c. protection of rights

3.2   worship

3.3   safe

3.4   God

3.5   Adult check

3.6   b

3.7   a

3.8   a

3.9   c

3.10 a

3.11 b

3.12 patriarch

3.13 tribal leader

3.14 judges

3.15 tribes

3.16 priests

3.17 The Ten Commandments

3.18 true

3.19 true

3.20 false

3.21 true

3.22 false

3.23 true

3.24 true

3.25 4
      1
      5
      3
      7
      6
      2

3.26 b

3.27 e

3.28 g

3.29 a

3.30 c

3.31 f

3.32 contrasts

3.33 compares

3.34 compares

3.35 compares

3.36 contrasts

3.37 Either order – examples:
      a. obey laws
      b. vote
      or, be alert to officials who are not
      doing a good job

3.38 Either order – examples:
      a. the right to vote
      b. freedoms of speech
      or, freedom of religion

SECTION ONE

1.1   Any order:
a. God is present everywhere
b. God is present everywhere at the
same time
c. God is a very personal God.

1.2   Example: It means that God is present
everywhere, in all places.

1.3   Any order:
a. love
b. truth
c. faithfulness
d. knowledge
e. power
f. holiness
g. goodness

1.4   all

1.5   Jeremiah

1.6   Isaiah

1.7   Either order:
a. The presence of God protected
David from Indians that were going
to kill him.
b. God protected David from a snake
that was going to bite him.

1.8   false

1.9   true

1.10   true

1.11   true

1.12   a

1.13   c

1.14   b

1.15   e

1.16   men

1.17   invisible

1.18   messenger

1.19   spirits

1.20   Either order:
a. evil spirits
b. demons

1.21   archangel

1.22   hosts

1.23   Any order:
a. pure spirits
b. real
c. personal
d. supernatural

1.24   Example: Angels are supernatural
because they can do many things that
people cannot do. They can quickly
travel from heaven to earth. They are
also much stronger and wiser than
men.

1.25   Any order:
a. speak to people
b. protect God's people
c. guide God's people
d. care for God's people

1.26   Adult check

1.27   true

1.28   true

1.29   true

1.30   false

1.31   true

1.32   false

1.33   true

1.34   Elijah

1.35   Jesus

1.36   Peter

1.37   ministering

1.38   Gabriel

1.39   angel

1.40   God

1.41   multitude, or host

1.42   true

1.43   false

1.44   false

1.45   true

SECTION TWO

2.1   Any order:
        a. It has one main and true author: God.
        b. It has one main theme: God's loving plan of salvation.
        c. It has one main character: Jesus Christ.
        d. It has one purpose: to reveal the Word of God and the plan of salvation to man.

2.2   c

2.3   a

2.4   c

2.5   b

2.6   a

2.7   c

2.8   a. The Bible
        b. Old Testament
        c. New Testament
        d. History
        e. Poetry
        f. Prophecy
        g. Gospels
        h. History
        i. Epistles
        j. Prophecy

2.9   Adult check

2.10   true

2.11   false

2.12   false

2.13   true

2.14   Either order:
        a. history
        b. prophecy

2.15   poetry

2.16   the Epistles

2.17   3

2.18   8

2.19   4

2.20   1

2.21   5

2.22   2

2.23   7

2.24   6

2.25   Any order:
        a. The Bible itself: it claims to be the Word of God.
        b. The characteristics of the Bible: one continuous story, unity, continuity, harmony
        c. Predictions fulfilled: the Bible contains prophecies that predict the future and were fulfilled.

2.26   Either order:
        a. history
        b. human experience

2.27   false

2.28   false

2.29   true

2.30   true

2.31 Either order:
a. physical science
b. life science

2.32 Example: The theory of evolution says that human life evolved from the simplest life forms in a "natural process" over millions of years.

2.33 Example: The theory of intelligent design tells us that the complexity of DNA molecules had to have an intelligent designer. That intelligent designer is God.

2.34 Example: Life science confirmed that many of the laws for healthy living in the Bible were correct in preventing illness and disease.

2.35 true

2.36 true

2.37 false

2.38 true

2.39 false

2.40 Any order:
a. The Bible as the Word of God, or the Bible's inspiration by God
b. God's Creation of the world
c. The Resurrection of Jesus Christ

2.41 James, Mary Magdalene, the apostles, five hundred, Paul, the disciples

2.42 fact

2.43 church

2.44 lives

SECTION THREE

3.1 faith

3.2 Friend

3.3 son, Isaac

3.4 God

3.5 blessed

3.6 "So then they which be of faith are blessed with faithful children."

3.7 false

3.8 true

3.9 false

3.10 true

3.11 Either order:
a. We must believe that He exists.
b. We must believe that He rewards those who earnestly seek Him.

3.12 David was obedient and wanted to do the will of god.

3.13 God was with him and blessed him.

3.14 Our fellowship with God is broken.

3.15 We should repent, confess our sins and ask God's forgiveness.

3.16 Any order:
a. a shepherd
b. a musician
c. a general
d. a soldier
e. a king
also, a friend, father

3.17 If we confess our sins, he is faithful and just, and will forgive our sins and cleanse us from all unrighteousness.

3.18 c

3.19 c

3.20 c

3.21 Example: God used Jonah to preach to the people, calling them to repent; and they repented.

3.22 Example: I can obey God and live for Him, and my life will be a witness for Him. I can also witness to my friends, neighbors and others and tell them about God's love for them and the Good News of Jesus Christ.

3.23 a. 2
b. 4
c. 1
d. 5
e. 3

3.24 Example: Paul loved God and worked hard to serve Him.

3.25 Adult check

3.26 true

3.27 false

3.28 true

3.29 true

3.30 always

3.31 strong

3.32 good

3.33 For to me to live is Christ, and to die is gain.

3.34 Adult check
1. d
2. e
3. k
4. i
5. c
6. h
7. m
8. j
9. f
10. a

3.35 loved

3.36 men

3.37 love

3.38 served

SECTION FOUR

4.1 God

4.2 Either order:
a. laws of nature
b. divine law

4.3 power

4.4 Jesus

4.5 d. a, b, and c

4.6 b. divine law

4.7 c. both a and b

4.8 true

4.9 true

4.10 true

4.11 Children, obey your parents in the Lord, for this is right.

4.12 Examples:
a. A patriarchal government is where a father of a family or household governs the family unit or household.
b. a tribal government is where a leader is chosen among men of a group of families or households.
c. A kingdom form of government exists where a king is chosen to govern over many tribes or a nation. It may be a full monarchy (the king has absolute rule) or a limited monarchy, where the king shares governing power with a parliament.
d. A democracy is a democratic republic where the people elect representatives to govern them.

4.13   God is the ultimate authority, and if a government commands us to do something against God's laws, we must obey God.

Examples: Adult check

4.14   b. religion

4.15   a. pray for

4.16   My son, hear the instruction of thy father, and forsake not the law of thy mother:

4.17   Any order:
a. love others
b. hear and obey instruction
c. receive correction
d. learn correct behavior

4.18   how you think

4.19   correct

4.20   duty, or responsibility

4.21   A new commandment I give unto you, That ye love one another; as I have loved you, that ye also love one another.

4.22   Any order:
a. love others
b. grow in Christ
c. give and receive support

4.23   Example: The church is like a family because it is the family of God. Other Christians in the church are our brothers and sisters in Christ. Like the family, our first duty in the church is to love others. Adult check

4.24   honestly and industriously

4.25   be a good loser and a graceful winner

4.26   be cheerful at all times

4.27   true

4.28   true

4.29   true

4.30   true

4.31   Doing things righteously

4.32   be honest and industrious

4.33   He that trusteth in his riches shall fall: but the righteous shall flourish as a branch.

4.34   eternity

4.35   soul

4.36   judgment

4.37   a. eternal life now
b. Heaven

4.38   a. fight
b. faith

4.39   For God so loved the world, that he gave his only begotten Son, that whosoever believeth in him should not perish, but have everlasting life.

SELF TEST 1

1.01   f

1.02   g

1.03   a

1.04   i

1.05   j

1.06   b

1.07   l

1.08   k

1.09   c

1.010   h

1.011   true

1.012   true

1.013   true

1.014   false

1.015   false

1.016   true

1.017   false

1.018   false

1.019   true

1.020   true

1.021   b

1.022   c

1.023   b

1.024   b

1.025   a

1.026   Jesus Christ

1.027   sacrifice

1.028   blessing

1.029   obedience *or* faith

1.030   repentance

1.031   Faith is the substance of things hoped for, the evidence of things not seen.

1.032   Example: The Jews honor Abraham as the father of the Hebrew nation. The Moslems honor him as their ancestor through Ishmael, the son of Abraham and Hagar, a slave woman. Christians honor Abraham for his faith in God and as an ancestor of Jesus Christ.

1.033   Example: David's heart was trustful, obedient, repenting, and worshipful.

1.034   Example: God tested Abraham's obedience by asking him to sacrifice his only son, Isaac. This would have been hard for Abraham because God had promised him that he would be the father of many nations and a blessing to the world through his children.

SELF TEST 2

2.01   k

2.02   f

2.03   i

2.04   e

2.05   h

2.06   m

2.07   l

2.08   c

2.09   d

2.010   a

2.011   true

2.012   true

2.013   false

2.014   false

2.015   false

2.016   true

2.017   false

2.018   true

2.019   false

2.020   true

2.021   true

2.022   false

2.023   true

2.024   false

2.025   true

2.026   Jesus Christ

2.027   Andrew

2.028   Gentile

2.029   fire

2.030   Mary

2.031   Barnabas

2.032   Lamb of God

2.033   heart

2.034   prisoner

2.035   five

2.036   Examples: Since Paul was born into a strict Jewish home, he would have learned the Old Testaments Scriptures well. Because of where he grew up (Tarsus), he became familiar with people of every class and race, and learned about different customs and languages.

2.037   Examples: John was among the first followers of Jesus. He was the only apostle present when Jesus was crucified. At the Cross, Jesus gave his mother, Mary, into the care of John. John was also the first apostle to believe in the Resurrection of Jesus when he outran Peter to the empty tomb.

SELF TEST 3

3.01   false

3.02   true

3.03   true

3.04   true

3.05   false

3.06   false

3.07   false

3.08   true

3.09   false

3.010 true

3.011 true

3.012 false

3.013 false

3.014 true

3.015 true

3.016 true

3.017 false

3.018 100

3.019 gleaner

3.020 ancestor

3.021 son

3.022 repented

3.023 thinking

3.024 martyr

3.025 The chapter tells of men and women who showed great faith in God. Because of their faith, these people pleased God.

3.026 Christians are encouraged to serve God faithfully. If we take our eyes off Jesus, we may lose the race. The goal of the race is Jesus.

3.027 He believed that God was able to raise Isaac from the dead.

3.028 Paul meant that his whole life was centered in Christ.

3.029 d

3.030 b

3.031 c

3.032 b

3.033 b

3.034 d

3.035 c

3.036 a

3.037 b

SELF TEST 1

1.01	e
1.02	f
1.03	h
1.04	g
1.05	a
1.06	k
1.07	b
1.08	l
1.09	c
1.010	j
1.011	false
1.012	true
1.013	false
1.014	false
1.015	true
1.016	true
1.017	true
1.018	false
1.019	true
1.020	true

1.021 a. sword of the Spirit/Word of God
b. helmet of salvation
c. shield of faith
d. breastplate of righteousness
e. belt of truth
f. gospel of peace

1.022	b
1.023	a
1.024	c
1.025	b
1.026	a

1.027 Any order:
a. Angels are spirits.
b. Angels are real.
c. Angels are personal.
d. Angels are supernatural.

1.028 invisible

1.029 real

1.030 temptation

1.031 ministering

1.032 Mary

1.033 Archangels, the angel hosts, and evil spirits are the kinds of angels mentioned in this LIFEPAC.

1.034 Angels think, sing, obey, plan, and show emotions. They are wise, can make choices, and can speak to people.

1.035 Just as the wind and electricity are real, even though we can't see them, so angels are real.

SELF TEST 2

2.01   d

2.02   f

2.03   g

2.04   k

2.05   i

2.06   l

2.07   e

2.08   a

2.09   c

2.010   b

2.011   Any order:
     a. Angels speak to people.
     b. Angels protect people.
     c. Angels guide people.
     d. Angels care for people.

2.012   Any order:
     a. Angels are spirits.
     b. Angels are real.
     c. Angels are personal.
     d. Angels are supernatural.

2.013   Any two:
     a. God provided food for Elijah
       through ravens.
     b. An angel provided food and water
       for Elijah in the wilderness.
     c. A widow provided food for Elijah.

2.014   false

2.015   false

2.016   false

2.017   true

2.018   false

2.019   true

2.020   true

2.021   true

2.022   true

2.023   true

2.024   cares

2.025   Egyptians

2.026   chains

2.027   Isaiah

2.028   12 legions of angels

2.029   Israel means "he contends with God."
     The Lord changed Jacob's name to
     Israel after Jacob had wrestled with the
     angel.

2.030   1. An angel freed Peter from prison.
     2. An angel protected Paul and the
       sailors during a storm at sea.
     3. An angel led Philip to the Ethiopian
       who accepted Jesus and was
       baptized.

SELF TEST 3

3.01   false

3.02   true

3.03   false

3.04   true

3.05   true

3.06   true

3.07   true

3.08   false

3.09   false

3.010 false

3.011 true

3.012 true

3.013 devil

3.014 quoting Scripture

3.015 strengthen

3.016 legions

3.017 fear

3.018 Any order:
a. Angels made announcements about Him.
b. Angels strengthened Him.
c. Angels accompanied Him back to heaven.

3.019 b

3.020 c

3.021 c

3.022 g

3.023 d

3.024 a

3.025 i

3.026 b

3.027 h

3.028 c

3.029 e

3.030 f

3.031 At least 1 from each time period.
Before:
The angel Gabriel appeared to Zacharias in the Temple and told him about the birth of his son, John the Baptist.
The angel Gabriel appeared to Mary and told her about the birth of her son, Jesus.
The angel of the Lord, probably Gabriel, appeared to Joseph and told him about the uniqueness of Mary's pregnancy.

During:
An angel appeared to the shepherds, announcing the birth and location of the Savior.

After:
An angel appeared to Joseph and told him to take his family and flee to Egypt.
An angel appeared to Joseph and told him to take his family back to Israel.

3.032 Any 3:
1. The angels waited on and strengthened Jesus after He was tempted by Satan in the desert.
2. Jesus was strengthened by an angel in the Garden of Gethsemane.
3. An angel rolled back the stone at Jesus' tomb and informed the two women that Jesus had risen.
4. Angels accompanied Jesus at His Ascension into Heaven.
5. After Jesus' Ascension, two angels spoke to Jesus' disciples about the Ascension and Jesus' second coming.

SELF TEST 1

1.01 true

1.02 true

1.03 false

1.04 false

1.05 true

1.06 true

1.07 false

1.08 true

1.09 false

1.010 true

1.011 omnipresence

1.012 person

1.013 true

1.014 promises

1.015 Any order:
a. love
b. know
c. obey

1.016 within

1.017 God is the same everywhere. Air is not the same everywhere.

1.018 God is omnipresent; present everywhere at the same time.

1.019 God thinks, speaks, commands, loves, and comforts.

1.020 Any five; any order:
a. love
b. faithfulness
c. knowledge
d. truth
e. power
f. holiness
g. goodness

1.021 O LORD, thou hast searched me, and known me. Thou knowest my downsitting and mine uprising, thou understandest my thought afar off.

1.022 I can only be in one place at a time.

1.023 He is beside, around, and within me. He is closer than breathing.

1.024 b

1.025 c

1.026 c

1.027 b

1.028 a

1.029 b

1.030 c

SELF TEST 2

2.01 sinned

2.02 Tabernacle

2.03 courage

2.04 wool

2.05 true

2.06 present

2.07 present

2.08 water

2.09 stopped

2.010 peace

2.011 f

2.012 d

2.013 e

2.014 a

2.015 b

2.016 true

2.017 true

2.018 false

2.019 false

2.020 true

2.021 false

2.022 false

2.023 false

2.024 true

2.025 true

2.026 Either order:
a. won many people to Christ
b. discovered many rivers and lakes

2.027 Any order:
a. loneliness
b. disease
c. wild animals

2.028 God was with him everywhere he went.

2.029 God helped her solve a prison riot. He was with her when Mrs. Lawson died. He helped her win many friends.

2.030 And Jesus came and spake unto them, saying, All power is given unto me in heaven and in earth. Go ye therefore, and teach all nations, baptizing them in the name of the Father, and of the Son, and of the Holy Ghost: Teaching them to observe all things whatsoever I have commanded you: and, lo, I am with you alway, even unto the end of the world. Amen.

SELF TEST 3

3.01	false	3.021	b
3.02	true	3.022	c
3.03	false	3.023	a
3.04	true	3.024	b
3.05	false	3.025	b
3.06	true	3.026	c
3.07	false	3.027	e
3.08	true	3.028	f
3.09	false	3.029	d or a
3.010	true	3.030	b

3.011   ear

3.012   eyes

3.013   death

3.014   God

3.015   animals

3.016   Any order:
a. through the Bible
b. through conscience
c. through the Holy Spirit

3.017   as far as the east is from the west

3.018   We should not forget the ways God provides for us. We should remember His goodness.

3.019   by guarding our lips

3.020   to trust God for all things
to let Him guide in everything

3.031   I love the LORD, because he hath heard my voice and my supplications. Because he hath inclined his ear unto me, therefore will I call upon him as long as I live.

SELF TEST 1

1.01	g
1.02	j
1.03	n
1.04	a
1.05	c
1.06	k
1.07	m
1.08	b
1.09	e
1.010	h
1.011	false
1.012	false
1.013	true
1.014	true
1.015	false
1.016	true
1.017	false
1.018	false
1.019	true
1.020	true
1.021	inspired
1.022	translated
1.023	twenty-seven
1.024	author
1.025	sin
1.026	b
1.027	c
1.028	a
1.029	b
1.030	c

1.031   Thy word is a lamp unto my feet, and a light unto my path.

1.032   God, who at sundry times and in divers manners spake in time past unto the fathers by the prophets, Hath in these last days spoken unto us by his Son, whom he hath appointed heir of all things, by whom also he made the worlds.

1.033   Example: It tells one continuous story. It is the most important book in the world ("the Book of books"). It is the largest selling book in the world. It was the first book printed (in 1455 by Johannes Gutenburg). It has been translated into more languages than any other book.

1.034   Example: It has basic unity of various parts in telling us the truth about God and man. It has one main author— God. It has one great theme—God's loving plan of salvation. It has one main character—Jesus Christ. It has one basic purpose—to reveal the Word of God and the plan of salvation to man.

SELF TEST 2

2.01	f	2.028	b
2.02	g	2.029	a
2.03	h	2.030	a
2.04	j	2.031	b
2.05	k	2.032	c

2.06   i

2.07   l

2.08   d

2.09   a

2.010   c

2.011   false

2.012   true

2.013   true

2.014   false

2.015   true

2.016   false

2.017   false

2.018   true

2.019   true

2.020   true

2.021   a. Genesis
       b. Exodus
       c. Leviticus
       d. Numbers
       e. Deuteronomy

2.022   a. Job
       b. Psalms
       c. Proverbs
       d. Ecclesiastes
       e. The Song of Solomon

2.023   b

2.024   a

2.025   b

2.026   a

2.027   c

2.033   This book of the law shall not depart out of thy mouth; but thou shalt meditate therein day and night, that thou mayest observe to do according to all that is written therein: for then thou shalt make thy way prosperous, and then thou shalt have good success.

2.034   Trust in the LORD with all thine heart; and lean not unto thine own understanding. In all thy ways acknowledge him, and he shall direct thy paths.

2.035   Example: Christ would be born of a virgin, visited by wise men, be taken to Egypt, be from the Tribe of Judah, be from the family of David, be announced by a forerunner, be poor, be born at a certain time and place.

2.036   Example: The prophets were men who spoke for God. Part of their work was to preach and teach God's Word. They also told people what would happen in the future. They were courageous men who warned the nation against serving false gods and called people back to the true God. Seventeen books of prophecy by Prophets are in the Old Testament.

SELF TEST 3

3.01   g

3.02   k

3.03   c

3.04   l

3.05   h

3.06   d

3.07   b

3.08   i

3.09   f

3.010   m

3.011   Synoptic

3.012   Vellum

3.013   he must be born again

3.014   church

3.015   Acts

3.016   false

3.017   false

3.018   true

3.019   false

3.020   true

3.021   true

3.022   false

3.023   true

3.024   false

3.025   false

3.026   5

3.027   2

3.028   1

3.029   4

3.030   3

3.031   For God so loved the world, that he gave his only begotten Son, that whosoever believeth in him should not perish, but have everlasting life.

3.032   But ye shall receive power, after that the Holy Ghost is come upon you: and ye shall be witnesses unto me both in Jerusalem, and in all Judaea, and in Samaria, and unto the uttermost part of the earth.

3.033   Example: When you accept Jesus as Savior, you become a child of God and are justified. This word means *just as if I'd never sinned*. God forgives all your sin. Because of what Jesus Christ has done for you, you are now able to stand in righteousness before God. God adds all of Christ's goodness to you.

SELF TEST 1

1.01   k

1.02   i

1.03   h

1.04   j

1.05   a

1.06   l

1.07   b

1.08   g

1.09   c

1.010   f

1.011   false

1.012   true

1.013   false

1.014   true

1.015   true

1.016   false

1.017   false

1.018   true

1.019   false

1.020   true

1.021   holy life

1.022   Wisdom

1.023   mercy, truth

1.024   outline

1.025   interact

1.026   a. of

1.027   c. obey

1.028   a. fear

1.029   b. nourished

1.030   b. example

1.031   Any order:
        a. home
        b. church
        c. school
        d. work

1.032   Any six of the following:
        a. is patient
        b. is kind
        c. is not jealous
        d. is not boastful
        e. is not arrogant
        f. is not rude
        g. does not insist on its own way
        h. is not irritable
        i. is not resentful
        j. does not rejoice at wrong
        k. rejoices in the right
        l. bears all things
        m. believes all things
        n. hopes all things
        o. endures all things

1.033   Train up a child in the way he should
        go: and when he is old, he will not
        depart from it.

SELF TEST 2

2.01	love one another	2.031	Any five of the following:

2.02 love

2.03 church

2.04 grow

2.05 holy life

2.06 neglect

2.07 Wisdom

2.08 instruction

2.09 interact

2.010 stability

2.011 false

2.012 true

2.013 true

2.014 true

2.015 false

2.016 true

2.017 true

2.018 true

2.019 true

2.020 false

2.021 h

2.022 j

2.023 i

2.024 k

2.025 a

2.026 l

2.027 g

2.028 b

2.029 f

2.030 e

2.031   Any five of the following:
a. love one another
b. not cause dissension
c. grow in Christ
d. be faithful to regular attendance when the church meets
e. receive instruction from ministers and teachers in the church
f. financially support the ministers and ministries of the church
g. help others in the church who are in need or want
h. use and exercise spiritual gifts

2.032   A new commandment I give unto you, That ye love one another; as I have loved you, that ye also love one another.

SELF TEST 3

3.01   e

3.02   j

3.03   f

3.04   h

3.05   i

3.06   b

3.07   l

3.08   c

3.09   a

3.010 d

3.011 false

3.012 true

3.013 false

3.014 false

3.015 true

3.016 false

3.017 true

3.018 false

3.019 false

3.020 true

3.021 true

3.022 false

3.023 My son, if sinners entice thee, consent thou not.

3.024 Example: by lying, by saying unkind things, by stirring up trouble

3.025 Even a child is known by his doings, whether his work be pure and whether it be right.

3.026 Examples: Making the attitude of your heart as if it were leaning forward to listen, wanting very much to understand or learn.

3.027 lying

3.028 medicine

3.029 Christ

3.030 humbly

3.031 gracefully

3.032 listen

3.033 love

3.034 Either order:
       a. attitudes
       b. actions

3.035 discipline

3.036 character

3.037 a. trust
       b. reverence

3.038 obeying

SELF TEST 4

4.01	c
4.02	i
4.03	g
4.04	d
4.05	m
4.06	b
4.07	h
4.08	k
4.09	f
4.010	l
4.011	understanding
4.012	sword
4.013	pleasant
4.014	yield
4.015	character
4.016	false
4.017	true
4.018	false
4.019	true
4.020	false
4.021	true
4.022	true
4.023	false
4.024	true
4.025	true
4.026	a. a fool
4.027	c. the Lord
4.028	d. Mary, the mother of Jesus
4.029	d. the Holy Spirit
4.030	b. trust

4.031 Example: A person's reputation is how he is known by other people. His reputation is how other people think he is. He usually gets his reputation from the way he acts and talks.

4.032 Example: People can show favoritism by giving jobs to people they like, treating some people more kindly, and giving better deals to people they like.

4.033 Example: God wants us to be diligent in our work, not lazy. Laziness does not fit the Christian life. Laziness in prayer, study, or in the work God has given you can hinder you from finding God's will.

SELF TEST 1

1.01	g
1.02	i
1.03	f
1.04	b
1.05	l
1.06	h
1.07	c
1.08	e
1.09	a
1.010	d
1.011	true
1.012	true
1.013	false
1.014	true
1.015	false
1.016	false
1.017	true
1.018	false
1.019	true
1.020	true

1.021 Example: Inspiration means the direct influence of God on the writers of the Bible. The Holy Spirit inspired the human writers of the Bible to write what He wanted them to write.

1.022 Example: It tells us that the Bible contains God's Word.

1.023 Bible prophecy can predict the future. God fulfills the prophecies.

1.024 Jesus Christ

1.025 The Bible grew, multiplied, and survived.

1.026 seed

1.027 lamp, or light

1.028 1,200

1.029 Christ's

1.030 Any order:
a. the Bible itself
b. history
c. human experience

1.031 Examples – any order:
a. His birth
b. His deity
c. His death
d. His Resurrection
e. His miracles

1.032 All scripture is given by inspiration of God, and is profitable for doctrine, for reproof, for correction, for instruction in righteousness: That the man of God may be perfect, throughly furnished unto all good works.

SELF TEST 2

2.01   h

2.02   g

2.03   i

2.04   a

2.05   j

2.06   l

2.07   b

2.08   f

2.09   k

2.010   c

2.011   true

2.012   true

2.013   false

2.014   false

2.015   true

2.016   true

2.017   false

2.018   true

2.019   false

2.020   true

2.021   b. God created

2.022   a. handiwork

2.023   b. sun

2.024   c. evil spirits

2.025   a. unclean

2.026   Theistic evolution

2.027   3,000

2.028   unknowns

2.029   Intelligent Design

2.030   His Word

2.031   Examples – any order:
a. They believe that the earth's atmosphere never changed. It was no different at the beginning of earth than it is now.
b. They believe in an unknown first life organism. This means that they do not know where life came from.
c. They believe in the theory that life began in the ocean. They cannot explain how or why life began in the ocean.
d. They believe that life evolved from simple life-form to the more complex. This is based on the idea that all life began from one simple organism.

2.032   Example: The Bible gives some rules and regulations that promote healthy living and sanitation. Many of these guidelines for healthy living have been confirmed scientific discoveries. For example, God forbade people to touch certain animals, and today we know these animals carry germs that can contaminate food and utensils. Also, these laws prevented the spread of communicable diseases.

SELF TEST 3

3.01	b		3.031	2
3.02	h		3.032	9
3.03	e		3.033	3
3.04	k		3.034	6
3.05	a		3.035	5
3.06	i		3.036	4
3.07	f		3.037	10
3.08	d		3.038	7
3.09	l		3.039	8
3.010	c		3.040	1
3.011	c			
3.012	a			
3.013	b			
3.014	a			
3.015	c			
3.016	predicted			
3.017	Resurrection			
3.018	Mary Magdalene			
3.019	Damascus			
3.020	Stephen			
3.021	false			
3.022	true			
3.023	false			
3.024	false			
3.025	false			
3.026	true			
3.027	true			
3.028	false			
3.029	true			
3.030	true			

SELF TEST 1

1.01	c	1.024	c
1.02	g	1.025	b
1.03	a	1.026	d
1.04	d	1.027	a
1.05	h	1.028	a
1.06	e	1.029	c
1.07	b	1.030	b
1.08	j	1.031	d
1.09	i	1.032	c
1.010	k	1.033	A
1.011	son of the commandment	1.034	B
1.012	a. law	1.035	F
	b. tentmaking	1.036	C
1.013	Stephen	1.037	D
1.014	Ananias	1.038	E

1.015   Jesus

1.016   Gentiles

1.017   three

1.018   Antioch

1.019   Holy Ghost

1.020   Any order:
Paul was a Roman citizen, a Pharisee, and had a proper education.

1.021   Any order:
The Jewish Law has a new purpose: to lead the sinner to Jesus.
Jesus was alive.

Paul was to preach to the Gentiles.

1.022   But sanctify the Lord God in your hearts: and be ready always to give an answer to every man that asketh you a reason of the hope that is in you with meekness and fear:

1.023   d

SELF TEST 2

2.01   g

2.02   j

2.03   i

2.04   k

2.05   d

2.06   c or f

2.07   a

2.08   b

2.09   h

2.010   e

2.011   Cyprus

2.012   Asia Minor

2.013   stoned

2.014   light

2.015   Roman citizen

2.016   strengthen

2.017   dream or vision

2.018   Mars

2.019   First, Paul would preach in the synagogues and then to the Gentiles. Then the Jews would persecute him. He would either be jailed or leave the city.

2.020   But sanctify the Lord God in your hearts: and be ready always to give an answer to every man that asketh you a reason of the hope that is in you with meekness and fear:

2.021   a. Was it right to preach to the Gentiles?
        b. Was it necessary for the Gentile believers to live strictly by the Jewish Law?

2.022   Paul was to continue his ministry and the Gentiles were asked to respect certain Jewish laws, but not all of them.

2.023   Antioch to Seleucia
        Seleucia to Salamis
        Salamis to Paphos
        Paphos to Perga
        Perga to Antioch of Pisidia
        Antioch to Iconium
        Iconium to Lystra
        Lystra to Derbe
        Derbe retraced to Perga
        Perga to Attalia
        Attalia to Antioch (Syria)

2.024   Antioch (Syria) to Tarsus
        Tarsus to Antioch (Pisidia)
          (through Derbe, Lystra, Iconium)
        Antioch to Galatia
        Galatia to Troas
        Troas to Philippi (through Neapolis)
        Philippi to Berea (through Thessalonica)
        Berea to Athens and Corinth
        Corinth to Ephesus
        Ephesus to Jerusalem (through Caesarea)
        Jerusalem to Antioch (Syria)
          (through Caesarea)

2.025   d

2.026   c

2.027   b

2.028   b

2.029   a

2.030   true

2.031   false

2.032   true

2.033   true

2.034   false

2.035   true

SELF TEST 3

3.01 Antioch (Syria) to Tarsus
Tarsus to Antioch (Pisidia)
  (via Derbe, Lystra, Iconium)
To Galatia
To Ephesus
To Philippi (via sea)
To Thessalonica
To Berea
To Corinth (via sea)
To Berea (via land)
To Thessalonica
To Philippi
To Troas (via Neapolis)
To Miletus (via an island)
To Patra (via Rhodes)
To Tyre
To Jerusalem (via Caesarea)

3.02 Jerusalem to Sidon (via land and sea)
Above Cyprus
To Myra
To Cnidus
To Fair Havens
To Clauda
To Syracuse
To Puteoli
To Rome (via land)

3.03 i

3.04 h

3.05 b

3.06 g

3.07 k

3.08 a

3.09 f

3.010 c

3.011 e

3.012 d

3.013 Because of Paul's teaching, few were buying the idols Demetrius made, and fewer tourists were visiting the town.

3.014 The Epistles written from Rome were Colossians, Philemon, Ephesians, Philippians, and 2 Timothy.

3.015 Paul's main emphasis in his preaching is "...Jesus Christ, and him crucified." (1 Corinthians 2:2)

3.016 We can witness. We can study the Bible. We can love one another.

3.017 Ephesus

3.018 crucified

3.019 Rome

3.020 Damascus

3.021 third

3.022 c

3.023 b

3.024 a

3.025 b

3.026 d

3.027 d

3.028 c

3.029 true

3.030 true

3.031 false

3.032 true

3.033 true

SELF TEST 1

1.01 Confess that Jesus is Lord and believe that Jesus rose from the dead. Ask Jesus to forgive your sins and accept Jesus as your Savior and live for Him.

1.02 A group of seventy-one Jewish scholars of the Mosaic Law who were responsible for the government of the Jewish community.

1.03 a member of the Sanhedrin (or, a Pharisee, ruler of the Jews, Jewish elder) who came to talk to Jesus at night

1.04 by being obedient to God and being controlled by Him; by following Jesus' example

1.05 the life of joy, blessing, and victory that God wants every Christian to have

1.06 e

1.07 a

1.08 f

1.09 c

1.010 b

1.011 Sanhedrin

1.012 soul

1.013 God

1.014 obedient

1.015 train

1.016 Christ

1.017 abundant

1.018 Paul

1.019 eternity

1.020 Holy Spirit

1.021 true

1.022 true

1.023 true

1.024 false

1.025 false

1.026 true

1.027 true

1.028 false

1.029 true

1.030 false

1.031 b

1.032 c

1.033 a

1.034 c

1.035 c

1.036 b

1.037 c

1.038 a

1.039 b

1.040 a

SELF TEST 2

2.01   false

2.02   true

2.03   true

2.04   true

2.05   false

2.06   false

2.07   true

2.08   false

2.09   true

2.010   true

2.011   c

2.012   b

2.013   b

2.014   a

2.015   b

2.016   b

2.017   c

2.018   c

2.019   c

2.020   b

2.021   A person can have eternal life by trusting Jesus as his personal Savior.

2.022   Nicodemus believed that Jesus was a teacher sent from God.

2.023   The Holy Spirit gives joy to the Christian. Our joy comes from knowing how much God loves us and what Jesus has done for us.

2.024   Christ will judge the works of Christians to determine the quality of their service to God. Christ will judge our motive for doing good.

2.025   Paul says that we should build our lives with gold, silver, and precious stones because these cannot be destroyed.

2.026   tangible

2.027   abundant

2.028   conscience

2.029   self-will

2.030   deed

2.031   judgment

2.032   refined

2.033   Jesus

2.034   hypocrites

2.035   feeding

SELF TEST 3

3.01 false

3.02 true

3.03 false

3.04 true

3.05 false

3.06 false

3.07 true

3.08 false

3.09 false

3.010 false

3.011 b

3.012 c

3.013 c

3.014 b

3.015 b

3.016 a

3.017 a

3.018 c

3.019 a

3.020 b

3.021 The unsaved will be judged from the Book of Life. Their names will not be written in the book, and they will be case into the lake of fire to spend eternity without God

3.022 In hell there will be darkness, weeping, and gnashing of teeth. Because God and Jesus will not be there, the residents of hell will spend an eternity without love, joy, and peace.

3.023 Any order:
a. God is perfect and just.
b. Man has a conscience to know right from wrong.

c. Man is responsible for his own choices.
or, God gave man a soul that will never die.

3.024 Any order:
a. The crown of life is for those who love God and endure temptation.
b. The crown of glory is for faithful ministers.
c. The crown of rejoicing is for soul winners.
d. The crown of righteousness is for those who love the appearing of Christ.

3.025 e

3.026 f

3.027 b

3.028 h

3.029 i

3.030 j

3.031 a

3.032 k

3.033 c

3.034 d

3.035 Patmos

3.036 abundant

3.037 Holy Spirit

3.038 eternity

3.039 train

3.040 dead

3.041 life

3.042 spiritual

SELF TEST 1

1.01	f	1.021	tempted
1.02	l	1.022	Father
1.03	g	1.023	Holy Spirit
1.04	b	1.024	witness
1.05	k	1.025	Mosaic
1.06	a	1.026	Instinct
1.07	j	1.027	Natural
1.08	e	1.028	Any order:
1.09	i		a. laws of nature
1.010	c		b. natural law
1.011	true		c. supernatural law
1.012	true	1.029	See illustration below.
1.013	true	1.030	Example: God has ultimate authority over all creation because He created everything that exists and He is all-powerful.
1.014	false		
1.015	true		
1.016	false	1.031	Example: The Holy Spirit strengthens us inwardly. He helps us to live the law of love and to live God's will, even when it is difficult.
1.017	true		
1.018	false		
1.019	true		
1.020	true		

1.029

GOD'S ETERNAL LAW

LAWS OF NATURE (INCLUDES *INSTINCT*)

DIVINE LAW (FOR PEOPLE)

NATURAL LAW (revealed in *nature*)

SUPERNATURAL LAW (revealed in the *Bible*)

SELF TEST 2

2.01	e	2.031	Jesus
2.02	j	2.032	parents
2.03	b	2.033	the Bible
2.04	m	2.034	easier
2.05	f	2.035	parents
2.06	a	2.036	c
2.07	k	2.037	c
2.08	h	2.038	c
2.09	l	2.039	b
2.010	d	2.040	c

2.011 false

2.012 true

2.013 false

2.014 false

2.015 true

2.016 false

2.017 true

2.018 true

2.019 false

2.020 true

2.021 false

2.022 false

2.023 true

2.024 true

2.025 false

2.026 obedience

2.027 image

2.028 God

2.029 responsibly

2.030 the Holy Spirit

2.041 Natural law is part of divine law. It is discovered by man through the things God has made.

2.042 Divine law is God's law for man and is revealed to us through natural law and supernatural law.

SELF TEST 3

3.01 g

3.02 j

3.03 d

3.04 a

3.05 e

3.06 c

3.07 k

3.08 i

3.09 b

3.010 f

3.011 God

3.012 family

3.013 tribes

3.014 Jesus

3.015 choose

3.016 a. Holy Spirit
       b. Pentecost

3.017 Creator

3.018 natural

3.019 divine

3.020 Holy Spirit

3.021 true

3.022 true

3.023 false

3.024 true

3.025 false

3.026 false

3.027 true

3.028 true

3.029 true

3.030 true

3.031 Either order:
       a. to obey laws
       b. to vote
       or, to be alert to government officials
       who are not doing a good job

3.032 a. God
       b. relatives
       c. father and mother
       d. sitters
       e. community
       f. children
       g. schools
       h. organizations
       i. churches

3.033 a

3.034 c

3.035 b

3.036 a

3.037 b

3.038 b

3.039 c

3.040 a

SELF TEST 1

1.01	d		1.031	Any five, any order:
1.02	c			a. love
1.03	j			b. truth
1.04	f			c. faithfulness
1.05	b			d. knowledge
1.06	i			e. power
1.07	a			f. holiness
1.08	e			g. goodness
1.09	k		1.032	false
1.010	g		1.033	false
1.011	everywhere		1.034	true
1.012	spirit		1.035	true
1.013	personal		1.036	true
1.014	all			
1.015	Holy Spirit			
1.016	messengers			
1.017	supernatural			
1.018	God			
1.019	protect			
1.020	ministering			
1.021	d			
1.022	c			
1.023	d			
1.024	c			
1.025	b			
1.026	c			
1.027	b			
1.028	c			
1.029	b			
1.030	d			

SELF TEST 2

2.01   d

2.02   g

2.03   a

2.04   e

2.05   b

2.06   c

2.07   h

2.08   i

2.09   j

2.010   k

2.011   true

2.012   false

2.013   true

2.014   true

2.015   true

2.016   false

2.017   true

2.018   false

2.019   true

2.020   true

2.021   d

2.022   d

2.023   b

2.024   b

2.025   c

2.026   d

2.027   c

2.028   d

2.029   b

2.030   b

2.031   Any order:
  a. It has one main and true author: God.
  b. It has one main theme: God's loving plan of salvation.
  c. It has one main character: Jesus Christ.
  d. It has one purpose: to reveal the Word of God and the plan of salvation to man.

2.032   Any one:

  a. the Bible itself
  b. history
  c. human experience

2.033   Example: The theory of intelligent design tells us that the complexity of DNA molecules had to have an intelligent designer. That intelligent designer is God.

2.034   Example: Life science confirmed that many of the laws for healthy living in the Bible were correct in preventing illness and disease.

SELF TEST 3

3.01	false
3.02	true
3.03	true
3.04	true
3.05	false
3.06	true
3.07	false
3.08	true
3.09	true
3.010	true
3.011	c
3.012	d
3.013	b
3.014	c
3.015	c
3.016	c
3.017	b
3.018	b
3.019	d
3.020	a

3.021 David was obedient and wanted to do the will of God.

3.022 God was with David and God blessed David.

3.023 Examples: He left his family to go to Canaan. He offered up his only son. He believed all of God's promises.

3.024 Examples: John was faithful to Christ and followed Him. At the Cross, John remained with Jesus' mother. John wrote five books in the Bible.

3.025 Any order:
a. the Bible itself
b. history
c. human experience

3.026 Any three, any order:
a. It has one main and true author: God.
b. It has one main theme: God's loving plan of salvation.
c. It has one main character: Jesus Christ.
d. It has one purpose: to reveal the Word of God and the plan of salvation to man.

3.027	presence, or angel
3.028	angels
3.029	Faith
3.030	Friend
3.031	3
3.032	8
3.033	1
3.034	4
3.035	6
3.036	9
3.037	2
3.038	5
3.039	7

SELF TEST 4

4.01   g

4.02   k

4.03   j

4.04   h

4.05   i

4.06   a

4.07   l

4.08   b

4.09   e

4.010   c

4.011   true

4.012   false

4.013   true

4.014   false

4.015   true

4.016   false

4.017   false

4.018   true

4.019   true

4.020   false

4.021   eternity

4.022   honest

4.023   love

4.024   Jesus Christ

4.025   Mosaic

4.026   one

4.027   c

4.028   c

4.029   d

4.030   c

4.031   c

4.032   Any order:
a. love others
b. hear and obey instruction
c. receive correction
d. learn correct behavior

4.033   For God so loved the world, that he gave his only begotten Son, that whosoever believeth in him should not perish, but have everlasting life.

4.034   Example: The church is like a family because it is the family of God. Other Christians in the church are our brothers and sisters in Christ. Like the family, our first duty in the church is to love others.

1. f
2. h
3. i
4. k
5. j
6. p
7. a
8. o
9. b
10. c
11. g
12. d
13. q
14. e
15. n
16. true
17. false
18. true
19. true
20. true
21. true
22. true
23. true
24. true
25. false
26. a
27. c
28. c
29. a
30. c

31. blessing
32. repentance
33. Lamb of God
34. witnesses
35. love one another
36. Faith is the substance of things hoped for, the evidence of things not seen.
37. David's heart was trusting, obedient, repentant, and worshipful.
38. John was among the first followers of Jesus. He was the only apostle present when Jesus was crucified. At the Cross, Jesus gave his mother, Mary, into the care of John. John was also the first apostle to believe in the Resurrection of Jesus when he outran Peter to the empty tomb.
39. Christians are encouraged to serve God faithfully. If we take our eyes off Jesus, we may lose the race. The goal of the race is Jesus.

1. e

2. g

3. f

4. a

5. b

6. i

7. l

8. k

9. j

10. h

11. false

12. true

13. false

14. true

15. true

16. true

17. true

18. false

19. true

20. true

21. a. Word of God
    b. salvation
    c. faith
    d. righteousness
    e. truth
    f. Gospel of peace

22. Any order:
    a. Angels are spirits.
    b. Angels are real.
    c. Angels are personal.
    d. Angels are supernatural.

23. Any order:
    a. Angels speak to people.
    b. Angels protect people.
    c. Angels guide people.
    d. Angels care for people.

24. b

25. b

26. c

27. a

28. b

29. a

30. Angels think, sing, obey, plan, and show emotions. They are wise, can make choices, and can speak to people.

31. Example: The angel Gabriel appeared to both Zacharias and Mary before the birth of Jesus. Also, an angel appeared to Joseph in a dream. An angel announced Jesus' birth to shepherds in Bethlehem, and then a host of angels appeared to them. An angel appeared to Joseph again in dreams after Jesus' birth.

32. Any 3:
    1. The angels waited on and strengthened Jesus after He was tempted by Satan in the desert.
    2. Jesus was strengthened by an angel in the Garden of Gethsemane.
    3. An angel rolled back the stone at Jesus' tomb and informed the two women that Jesus had risen.
    4. Angels accompanied Jesus at His Ascension into Heaven.
    5. After Jesus' Ascension, two angels spoke to Jesus' disciples about the Ascension

33. 1. An angel freed Peter from prison.
    2. An angel protected Paul and the sailors during a storm at sea.
    3. An angel led Philip to the Ethiopian who accepted Jesus and was baptized.

1. true
2. false
3. true
4. false
5. false
6. true
7. true
8. false
9. true
10. false
11. person
12. faithful
13. Tabernacle
14. water
15. body
16. Examples; any order:
    a. love
    b. truth
    c. knowledge
17. Any order:
    a. Gideon
    b. Joshua
    c. David
18. Any order:
    a. David Brainerd
    b. David Livingstone
    c. Gladys Aylward
19. Any order:
    a. through the Bible
    b. through conscience
    c. through the Holy Spirit
20. b
21. a
22. c
23. b
24. d
25. c
26. g
27. h
28. f
29. a
30. Adult check
31. And Jesus came and spake unto them, saying, All power is given unto me in heaven and in earth. Go ye therefore, and teach all nations, baptizing them in the name of the Father, and of the Son, and of the Holy Ghost: Teaching them to observe all things whatsoever I have commanded you: and, lo, I am with you alway, even unto the end of the world. Amen.

1. f
2. h
3. j
4. g
5. i
6. l
7. k
8. c
9. e
10. a
11. false
12. true
13. true
14. true
15. true
16. false
17. true
18. false
19. false
20. true
21. inspired
22. twenty-seven
23. author
24. Synoptic
25. he must be born again
26. Thy word is a lamp unto my feet, and a light unto my path.
27. Trust in the LORD with all thine heart; and lean not unto thine own understanding. In all thy ways acknowledge him, and he shall direct thy paths.
28. For God so loved the world, that he gave his only begotten Son, that whosoever believeth in him should not perish, but have everlasting life.

29. a. Job
    b. Psalms
    c. Proverbs
    d. Ecclesiastes
    e. The Song of Solomon

30. a. Romans
    b. 1 Corinthians
    c. 2 Corinthians
    d. Galatians
    e. Ephesians

31. Example: It tells one continuous story. It is the most important book in the world ("the Book of books"). It is the largest selling book in the world. It was the first book printed (in 1455 by Johannes Gutenburg). It has been translated into more languages than any other book.

32. Example: Christ would be born of a virgin, visited by wise men, be taken to Egypt, be from the Tribe of Judah, be from the family of David, be announced by a forerunner, be poor, be born at a certain time and place.

33. Example: When you accept Jesus as Savior, you become a child of God and justified. This word means just-as-if-I'd never sinned. God forgives all your sin. Because of what Jesus Christ has done for you, you are now able to stand in righteousness before God. God adds all of Christ's goodness to you.

1. e
2. f
3. h
4. j
5. i
6. l
7. k
8. c
9. d
10. b
11. true
12. false
13. true
14. false
15. true
16. true
17. false
18. true
19. false
20. true
21. wisdom
22. holy life
23. sword
24. character
25. medicine
26. neglect
27. instruction
28. stability
29. humbly
30. Grow

31. Train up a child in the way he should go: and when he is old, he will not depart from it.

32. A new commandment I give unto you, That ye love one another; as I have loved you, that ye also love one another.

33. Example: Apply means to put to some practical use. You must really listen to teachers and other students in order to understand the meaning of what you hear, then practice the things you learn. Applying what you learn will help you to remember and will make you a better student.

34. Example: Laziness does not fit the Christian life. The Book of Proverbs has many verses that tell of the benefits of work as well as the penalties of laziness.

1. e
2. g
3. f
4. h
5. a
6. j
7. l
8. b
9. k
10. i
11. true
12. true
13. true
14. true
15. false
16. false
17. true
18. true
19. true
20. true
21. seed
22. lamp, or light
23. Christ's
24. unknowns
25. intelligent design
26. His Word
27. Resurrection
28. Mary Magdalene
29. Damascus
30. Stephen
31. Examples – any order:
    a. They believe that the earth's atmosphere never changed. It was no different at the beginning of earth than it is now.
    b. They believe in an unknown first life organism. This means that they do not know where life came from.
    c. They believe in the theory that life began in the ocean. They cannot explain how or why life began in the ocean.
    d. They believe that life evolved from simple life-form to the more complex. This is based on the idea that all life began from one simple organism.
32. Any five of the following – any order:
    a. Mary Magdalene
    b. Two women at tomb
    c. Two disciples on the road to Emmaus
    d. Peter
    e. The disciples with Peter
    f. Thomas
    g. Seven disciples by the Sea of Tiberius
    h. Five hundred brethren
    i. James
    j. Apostles at the Ascension
    k. Paul
    l. Stephen
33. All scripture is given by inspiration of God, and is profitable for doctrine, for reproof, for correction, for instruction in righteousness: That the man of God may be perfect, throughly furnished unto all good works.

1. j
2. i
3. f
4. g
5. k
6. h
7. d
8. e
9. b
10. a
11. Antioch to Seleucia
   Seleucia to Salamis
   Salamis to Paphos
   Paphos to Perga
   Perga to Antioch of Pisidia
   Antioch to Iconium
   Iconium to Lystra
   Lystra to Derbe
   Derbe retraced to Perga
   Perga to Attalia
   Attalia to Antioch (Syria)
12. d
13. c
14. d
15. b
16. Ananias
17. Gentiles
18. tentmaking
19. Mars
20. Sergius Paulus
21. three
22. beheaded
23. Achaia
24. crucified
25. Christ

26. a. 4
   b. 3
   c. 2
   d. 5
   e. 1
27. a. He was a Roman citizen
   b. He was a Jewish Pharisee.
   c. He had a good education. (or He knew both the Greek and Hebrew languages.)
   d. He was trained by God after receiving God's call.
28. But sanctify the Lord God in your hearts: and be ready always to give an answer to every man that asketh you a reason of the hope that is in you with meekness and fear:

1. i
2. c
3. e
4. k
5. j
6. a
7. b
8. d
9. h
10. f
11. b. born again
12. a. love
13. b. patience
14. c. the world
15. c. Christ
16. b. fire
17. c. Jesus
18. a. the living and the dead
19. c. destruction
20. b. hell
21. false
22. true
23. false
24. false
25. false
26. false
27. true
28. false
29. true
30. true
31. true
32. Holy Spirit
33. asleep
34. Paul
35. destroyed
36. crowns
37. minister
38. just
39. conscience
40. quality
41. love
42. Any order:
    a. The crown of life – for those who love God and endure temptation
    b. The crown of glory – for faithful ministers
    c. The crown of rejoicing – for soul winners
    d. The crown of righteousness – for those who love Christ's appearing
43. Example: There will be darkness, weeping, and gnashing of teeth. God and Jesus will not be there so the residents of hell will spend eternity without love, joy, and peace.

1. c
2. g
3. f
4. i
5. a
6. l
7. k
8. b
9. j
10. e
11. true
12. true
13. true
14. true
15. false
16. true
17. true
18. true
19. true
20. true

21. tempted
22. Mosaic
23. Natural
24. parents
25. family
26. patriarch
27. limited
28. a. God
    b. relatives
    c. father and mother
    d. sitters
    e. community
    f. children
    g. schools
    h. organizations
    i. churches
29. See illustration below.
30. Example: God has ultimate authority over all creation because He created everything that exists and He is all-powerful.
31. Example: Governments are needed for order, safety, and the protection of rights. Chaos, confusion, and anxiety would result if there were no government.

29.

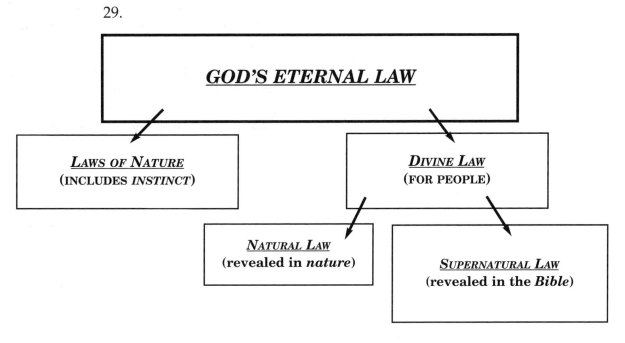

1. g
2. h
3. j
4. a
5. i
6. b
7. k
8. l
9. c
10. f
11. false
12. true
13. true
14. true
15. true
16. true
17. true
18. true
19. true
20. true
21. omnipresent
22. supernatural
23. industrious
24. love
25. Faith
26. d
27. b
28. b
29. c
30. d

31. a. Any one of these: Genesis, Exodus, Leviticus, Numbers, Deuteronomy, Joshua, Judges, Ruth, 1 Samuel, 2 Samuel, 1 Kings, 2 Kings, 1 Chronicles, 2 Chronicles, Ezra, Nehemiah, Esther
    b. Acts
    c. Any one of these: Job, Psalms, Proverbs, Ecclesiastes, Song of Solomon
    d. Any one of these: Romans, 1 Corinthians, 2 Corinthians, Galatians, Ephesians, Philippians, Colossians, 1 Thessalonians, 2 Thessalonians, 1 Timothy, 2 Timothy, Titus, Philemon, Hebrews, James, 1 Peter, 2 Peter, 1 John, 2 John, 3 John, Jude
    e. Any one of these: Isaiah, Jeremiah, Lamentations, Ezekiel, Daniel, Hosea, Joel, Amos, Obadiah, Jonah, Micah, Nahum, Habakkuk, Zephaniah, Haggai, Zechariah, Malachi

32. Any order:
    a. physically
    b. mentally
    c. spiritually

33. Either order:
    a. Heaven
    b. Hell

34. Example: Life science confirmed that many of the laws for healthy living in the Bible were correct in preventing illness and disease.

35. Example: There are mainly four things that angels do to help people. They speak to people, protect God's people, guide God's people, and care for God's people.